KNIT, PRAY, SHARE

LISA HENNESSY

HARVEST HOUSE PUBLISHERS
EUGENE, OREGON

Cover by Emily Weigel Design

Cover photo © Melica / Shutterstock

Photo on page 90 © galinka_zhi / Fotolia

All other photography by Jay Eads

Interior design and production by Dugan Design Group

KNIT, PRAY, SHARE

Copyright © 2019 by Lisa Hennessy
Published by Harvest House Publishers
Eugene, Oregon 97408
www.harvesthousepublishers.com

ISBN 978-0-7369-7819-4 (pbk.)
ISBN 978-0-7369-7820-0 (eBook)

Library of Congress Cataloging-in-Publication Data

Names: Hennessy, Lisa, author.
Title: Knit, pray, share / Lisa Hennessy.
Description: Eugene, Oregon : Harvest House Publishers, 2019.
Identifiers: LCCN 2018061519 (print) | LCCN 2019000560 (ebook) | ISBN
   9780736978200 (ebook) | ISBN 9780736978194 (pbk.)
Subjects: LCSH: Knitting—Patterns. | Knitters (Persons)—Prayers and
   devotions.
Classification: LCC TT825 (ebook) | LCC TT825 .H46 2019 (print) | DDC
   746.43/2—dc23
LC record available at https://lccn.loc.gov/2018061519

Printed in China

19 20 21 22 23 24 25 26 27 / RDS-DDG / 10 9 8 7 6 5 4 3 2 1

ACKNOWLEDGMENTS

First and foremost, I have to thank my heavenly Father for the inspiration and guidance for writing this book. I also thank Him for all of my family and friends who have been so supportive of this endeavor.

Of course, none of this would have been possible without my husband's love and support with all of my writing and knitting.

I have had many people praying me through this. I wish I could list and thank every person who has been instrumental in this journey, but I fear I would unknowingly leave someone off the very long list of thank-yous. However, I would be remiss if I didn't give special thanks to my knitting friends: Mary Dahms, for helping me proof and knit these patterns, and Patti Delsandro, who not only helped me knit some of these projects but also assisted with some of the pattern designs. My daughter, Danielle, was a huge help with some of my editing as well as helping with the videos on my YouTube channel. My dear friend Carla from graduate school has been through this process with me a few times, and I cherish her editing skills, as well as my sister-in-law, Sonia, who has been a sounding board during this entire book process.

I am so thankful for both Harvest House and my agent, Adria Goetz, for believing in me and my mission of sharing God's love through knitting. None of this would have been possible without them sharing this vision.

—Lisa Hennessy

Contents

HATS AND HEADBANDS

BABY GIFTS

BAGS AND TOTES

PETS

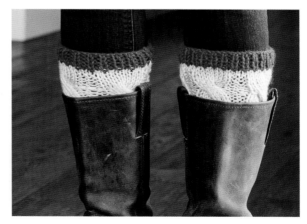

WHY ME? WHY KNITTING?

While this book is about knitting and making a difference in God's kingdom, it's also about more than that. Even though I grew up in the church and considered myself a Christian, I really didn't know who Jesus was. Unfortunately, it took a tragedy for me to realize this.

At the age of 28, I unexpectedly became a pregnant, widowed single mom. During that dark time in my life, I discovered a faith I didn't know I had. God turned my pain into purpose and my hurt into hope. Restored by the loving hand of my Lord and Savior, I went from being a broken, hopeless widow to a child of God as He transformed the painful pieces of my life into beautiful blessings, including remarriage to a wonderful husband and father to my children.

One of the ways God brought beauty out of my ashes was through knitting. Because of my grief journey, once I became more proficient with this skill, God gave me a desire to make prayer shawls to give to others who were broken and hurting. From there, I began to knit more gifts and share them with others. And I began to think of ways that more people could join me on this knitting journey.

Part of my passion for sharing my knitting was inspired by our world's "disconnect." Knitting keeps me from being mindlessly enslaved to my phone. It reminds me to focus on not just what I am making, but it also allows me time to pray about the person for whom I am creating something. Not only does the act of knitting help me reflect internally, but it also causes me to engage with the people around me, whether they are other knitters or just individuals inquiring about my work. My craft allows me the opportunity to start conversations and build connections.

When I'm with a group knitting at a coffee house, other customers around us may be connected to the Wi-Fi, but we are connected to one another. Knitting allows us to do something with our hands besides scrolling on our smartphones. I believe God gave me this creative passion for a purpose: to share His love through my hands and heart. I love how knitting helps me take the focus off myself by redirecting my energy toward making gifts that will bless others.

I find that when I make myself turn away from all of the distractions of the world, I am able to more clearly see and experience the moments God has handcrafted for me to enjoy, including fellowship with others in the knitting community. As a Christian, I so appreciate God's reminders for me to look beyond myself to what really matters eternally.

This book is designed for knitters of all skill levels, with an emphasis on less-complicated creations. I've noted the different skill levels recommended for each project. The majority of the patterns in this book are level 1 or 2.

♡ = simple
♡ ♡ ♡ ♡ = advanced

For any unfamiliar techniques, please refer to my "Knitting Tutorials" tab at KnitPrayShare.com, where you see this ▧ symbol in the instructions.

Here, I have both my own tutorials as well as links to other experts. Additionally, if you are a loose knitter, I would recommend going down a needle size from my recommendations.

I am the garter-stitch queen, so if you are an avid, proficient knitter who likes to be challenged by different stitch variations, please don't be deterred by the simplicity of most of these patterns. Personally, I can't carry on a conversation in public if I have to follow any kind of pattern outside of the garter or stockinette stitch. The patterns in this book are fairly easy and don't require a lot of skill or concentration. With the exception of a few items, I intentionally picked fast-knit projects that will fit into our fast-paced lifestyles.

And while I often enjoy challenging patterns, quick and easy projects are a welcome break when I am working on something more complicated.

Also, simple patterns allow more people to knit together in groups and to complete more projects to share with others.

For easy reference you will find a key for all the abbreviations used in the patterns on the inside front cover and back cover.

Every project has red yarn at the beginning and end of it. This is what makes our projects unique. The red symbolizes Christ's blood shed for us. Having some shade of red or pink at the top and bottom of your gift signifies how we are all sealed with the blood of Christ from the beginning to the end. "Knit, pray, share" signifies that as you knit your gift, you will be thanking God and praying for the person who will receive your hand-knit item.

You'll find a suggestion for a Scripture to include on a gift tag at the end of each pattern. Consider including the following little note which suggests what to do if the gift made a difference in the recipient's day. Those who receive these hand-knit creations can use the hashtag #KnitPrayShare after they receive the gift, when they post on Facebook, Instagram, or Twitter. One random gift of kindness from *Knit, Pray, Share* can spread smiles across the world.

This gift was prayed over for you. If it made a difference in your day, consider being part of the movement and posting a picture on social media using the hashtag #KnitPrayShare.

Felting Instructions

Not all fibers can be felted. In general, animal fibers—with the exception of silk—felt well. Wool, mohair, alpaca, cashmere, and llama are some examples of fiber that easily felts. Always read labels to make sure your yarn of choice isn't "superwash," because it won't felt if it's been treated.

The easiest way to felt is to use a washing machine that has an agitator. If you don't have one, a local laundromat might.

Before washing, place your item to be felted in a mesh zippered laundry bag or pillowcase. (Knot the top of the pillowcase to contain your project.) Put your project in the washing machine with a small amount of detergent and throw in some old towels or jeans to assist in the felting process. Set your washing machine to the hottest setting and the heaviest cycle. Check your item every 10 minutes or so until your item reaches the desired size. From my experience, larger pieces, such as bags, normally take the whole cycle. If it's still too big after washing, either rewash it or place the item in the dryer to continue the shrinking process.

Another option, if you have the space to store and the muscle to use it, is a countertop, hand-cranked washing machine. You can easily find these online.

I usually wait until I have completed several items before I go to the laundromat. This is the quickest and most cost-effective way for me to felt them, and I can sit and knit while I am waiting!

Care instructions for all finished felted projects should be to hand-wash in cold water and air dry.

Hats and Headbands

Chemo Do-Rag
14

Chunky Knit Hat
with Pom-Pom
16

Homeless Loom
Knit Hat with Brim
18

Twisted Rib Skull Hat
22

Slouchy Seed Stitch Hat
26

Ear Warmer/Headband
30

CHEMO DO-RAG

Unfortunately, many of us have been touched by cancer, whether the disease has affected a friend, a family member, or us personally. In fact, even as I sat down to write this pattern, I heard my phone ding with a text from my sister-in-law, who was recently diagnosed with stage 4 breast cancer. I've made her two of these do-rags in an amazing bamboo yarn I bought at one of the local yarn shops. She was very appreciative because the wig she had ordered was on back order. Plus, this bamboo yarn (or a light cotton) would feel much cooler than any wig in our 100-degree Texas summers.

When I hear of someone who is about to undergo chemotherapy, this is my go-to project. It's a quick, easy, tangible way to show love for the person and convey that you are there for them. When you give this gift, consider adding some other items to the gift bag. Do you have a favorite book you'd like to share with them? What about an online gift card so they can download music or audiobooks to listen to while undergoing treatment?

SKILL LEVEL ♡ ♡

MATERIALS

Size US 7 (4.5 mm) 36-inch circular needle

Size G crochet hook

1 skein of bamboo or cotton yarn in red

1 skein of bamboo or cotton yarn for the main color*

I used a hand-dyed bamboo yarn called Makimo from FiberLady.com.

CARE INSTRUCTIONS

Hand-wash in cold water or wash on cold, delicate cycle; lay flat to dry.

DIRECTIONS

With red yarn, CO 120 stitches.

Row 1: K.

Row 2: Switch to MC and K. Mark this as the right side of the piece.

Row 3: K1, K2tog, K until the last 3 stitches, K2tog, K1.

Row 4: K.

Repeat rows 3 and 4 until 5 stitches are left on the needle.

Cut the yarn and pull the tail through those last 5 stitches, weaving in the ends. Using the red yarn, SC both sides of the triangle. ◼ Attach a gift tag.

The human spirit can endure in sickness, but a crushed spirit who can bear?

Proverbs 18:14

Dear Lord, I pray for the person who will receive this gift to not let cancer crush her spirit. Surround her with loving family and friends who will lift her up when she can't bear the pain. Despite her diagnosis, Lord, I pray she feels all of the intercessory prayers being made on her behalf. I ask that each time she wears this do-rag, she is reminded that You see her beauty. It is in the name of Jesus that I pray these things. Amen.

Chunky Knit Hat with Pom-Pom

With the onslaught of social media, self-perception can become warped—especially in the population of teen and preteen girls. The world tells them that outer beauty is what matters most, but God's Word tells us that our inner self is what should shine (see 1 Peter 3:3-4). Can you think of a girl who needs to be reminded she is beautiful in God's eyes?

Perhaps a young lady you see at church or in your neighborhood is struggling to see her own self-worth. Or a family member or daughter of a friend doesn't believe in her own beauty. What would happen if you not only prayed for her, but also let her know that you noticed and admired her beautiful soul and spirit? When you give her this hat, you can let her know she is worthy and loved. Many young girls need this important affirmation, and your kind words and prayers could be exactly what she needs to boost her self-confidence and allow her to see herself as God sees her.

SKILL LEVEL ♡ ♡

MATERIALS

Size US 19 (15 mm) straight needles

Chunky yarn, red*

Chunky yarn for main color*

Scissors

Tapestry needle

Large or jumbo pom-pom maker

*I used Hobby Lobby's Yarn Bee Uber Luxe for both yarn colors.

CARE INSTRUCTIONS

Machine wash in cold water, delicate cycle; air dry.

DIRECTIONS

CO 24 stitches in red.

K2P2 for 4 inches for the cuff. Switch to MC. Continue K2P2 until the piece measures 11 inches from the beginning.

Once you have reached the desired length, you will start your decrease by K2tog to the end of the row.

Cut the yarn long enough to pull through the remaining stitches and cinch the top of the hat closed.

Using the mattress stitch, you may now sew up the sides. ◼️◀

Make a red pom-pom for the top using either the large or jumbo pom-pom maker. I used the jumbo for mine because everything is bigger in Texas!

Attach pom-pom to the top of the hat. Attach a gift tag.

Don't be concerned about the outward beauty of fancy hairstyles, expensive jewelry, or beautiful clothes. You should clothe yourselves instead with the beauty that comes from within, the unfading beauty of a gentle and quiet spirit, which is so precious to God.

1 Peter 3:3-4 NLT

Dear Lord, I pray that this young lady sees her worth in You and doesn't let the world's definition of beauty define her. Remove any negative thoughts or feelings that cause her to not see herself as "good enough." Lift up her spirits when she is down. Bless her with godly friendships and mentors who will affirm her beautiful, loving soul. It is in the name of Jesus that I pray these things. Amen.

HOMELESS LOOM
KNIT HAT WITH BRIM

W hen people find out that I knit, inevitably many of them give me yarn they have lying around the house that they have no use for. Usually the yarn that I have given to me is more of a craft store type of yarn. Don't get me wrong; I truly appreciate the donations. But I don't usually use this yarn for myself.

I am not a yarn snob by any means, but I am particular about which yarns I like to use for specific projects. For loom knit hats, I actually prefer yarns such as Red Heart Super Saver or Hobby Lobby's I Love This Yarn. These are good yarns to use double strands (knitting with two strands of yarn as one) to make hats on the knitting loom.

Not only is this a good way for me to use hand-me-down yarn, but it's also a quick way to make several hats to donate to homeless shelters. Keep one in your car for cold days when you see someone with a sign asking for money or food. You can give them a homemade knit hat along with something to eat and drink.

SKILL LEVEL ♡♡

MATERIALS

36-peg round loom*

1 skein worsted weight acrylic yarn, red

1 skein worsted weight acrylic yarn, coordinating color, for main color

Loom hook

Yarn needle

Pom-pom maker, your choice for size

I used the green Knifty Knitter loom.

CARE INSTRUCTIONS

Machine wash in cool or warm water, delicate cycle; tumble dry on low or air dry.

DIRECTIONS

This will be made using the e-wrap stitch.

To make the cuff, using double strands of the red yarn, make a slip knot on the outer peg that is on the edge of the loom. Wrap the yarn around the pegs going to the right (counterclockwise, called the e-wrap stitch). Push the stitches toward the bottom and wrap a second time around. Using your loom hook, take the bottom row and lift over the top row on each peg. When you are finished, you will be back to having one row; push the stitches toward the bottom of the peg and rewrap. If you want a 2-inch brim, continue in the red for 4 inches.

Once you have reached 4 inches (make sure there is only one row of loops on your pegs when you do this), cut one strand of your red yarn, leaving about a 4-inch tail. From your cast-on row, find the stitch closest to that first peg (to the right of the outer peg where you put the slip knot). Take that stitch and pull it on the peg that lines up with that stitch. Work your way around by grabbing the next stitch and pulling onto the next peg. Continue until you are all the way around the loom with 2 rows of yarn on each peg. 🎥

Pull the bottom row over the top row. The top loop is pretty loose, so be careful when you are pulling that bottom row over the top row so that it doesn't slip off the loom. When you are finished, cut the red yarn, leaving enough yarn to be able to weave in those ends. You are now finished with the cuff of the hat.

Change to MC yarn. You can pull off the slip knot of the red yarn and put a slip knot with the color change on the outer peg. Continue wrapping the MC yarn as you did with the red yarn until your piece from top to bottom measures about 8 to 9 inches from the brim. Eight inches makes it more of a beanie. For a looser hat, knit for 9 inches.

Once your piece measures 8 to 9 inches, with one row of yarn on the pegs, cut your yarn long enough to pull through all of the stitches. (I usually wrap the yarn once around the loom and cut it that length.) Thread the yarn tail through your yarn needle. Starting with the first peg and moving counterclockwise, use the needle to sew through the yarn loop on each peg. Once you have pulled the yarn and needle through that stitch, slip it off of the loom. Continue to do this until you get to the end.

Turn your hat inside out. Pull the two ends of your yarn together to cinch up the material at the top of your hat; sew to anchor shut. Leave the yarn hanging so you can tie your pom-pom down with that yarn.

Make a red pom-pom and attach to the top of the hat. (I used the medium size pom-pom maker for the one in the photo.)

Share your food with the hungry, and give shelter to the homeless. Give clothes to those who need them, and do not hide from relatives who need your help.

Isaiah 58:7 NLT

Dear Lord, I thank You for generous donations and inexpensive yarn that enable me to make hats for people less fortunate than I am. I pray for those who are living on the streets without a roof over their heads. Lord, lead them to strong Christians who can draw them to You and Your supernatural, divine healing. Despite the cold weather, when they put this hat on their head, I pray that they be reminded of the love and comfort that You provide for them. It is in the name of Jesus that I pray these things. Amen.

Twisted Rib Skull Hat

While I was making this hat, I had in mind that I wanted to give it to a crossing guard, church volunteer, or police officer who was directing parking lot traffic. I know that at our church, regardless of the weather, I see the same people volunteering every Sunday to help manage the traffic before and after church services. They truly live Romans 12:11: "Never be lacking in zeal, but keep your spiritual fervor, serving the Lord."

Even though I live in Texas, we still have plenty of cold and windy days where this hat could be worn. I'd love to be able to eventually bless each parking crew volunteer with one of these hats. In fact, making them would be a great group project for my knitting circle.

These skull hats are something you could easily give to any outdoor volunteer in your local community, such as the school crossing guards. While they may get paid to do this service, they usually don't make much money. Many invest their time because they want to keep children safe and out of harm's way. This gift is a simple way to let them know how much you appreciate what they do.

SKILL LEVEL ♡ ♡ ♡

MATERIALS

Size US 8 (5mm) 16-inch circular needle

4 size US 8 (5mm) double-pointed needles

1 skein worsted weight yarn, your choice for main color*

Worsted weight yarn, red*

Stitch marker

Row counter

Yarn needle

*I used I Love This Yarn from Hobby Lobby

DIRECTIONS

Using the circular needle and red yarn, CO 80 stitches. This hat is worked in a 1 x 1 twisted rib stitch, knitting in the rnd. 🎥

Rnds 1-5: K in red in the twisted rib pattern.

Rnd 6: Switch to MC yarn and continue knitting the twisted rib pattern until your piece measures 4 inches from your CO edge.

Rnds 7-10: Switch to red yarn and K using the twisted rib pattern for 4 rnds.

Switch to MC and continue knitting in twisted rib pattern until the piece measures 7 inches from the beginning.

Switch back to the red yarn to start your decrease rnds.

Decrease rnds

Note: Switch to double-pointed needles when it becomes too difficult to continue knitting with your circular needle.

Rnd 1: Continuing to K in twisted rib pattern, *K1P1, K2tog* to end of rnd. (Make sure you are putting your needle in the back of the stitches when you do the K2tog decreases.) (60 stitches)

CARE INSTRUCTIONS

Machine wash in cool or warm water; air dry or tumble dry on low heat.

Rnd 2: Continue knitting in the twisted rib pattern, working each stitch either K or P as it appears.

Rnd 3: Same as Rnd 2 to last stitch; move this stitch to your first needle without working.

Rnd 4: (Second decrease rnd) *K2tog, P1* to end of rnd. (40 stitches)

Rnds 5-6: K 2 rnds in the twisted rib stitch.

Rnd 7: (Third decrease rnd) K2tog to end of rnd. (20 stitches)

Leaving a long tail, cut yarn. Using your yarn needle, thread the yarn through the remaining stitches and draw up tightly.

Turn the hat inside out, secure the end, and weave in all yarn ends. Attach a gift tag.

Note: If you are using yarn such as Hobby Lobby's I Love This Yarn, you will have enough yarn left over to make a matching scarf using this same 1 x 1 twisted rib pattern. Using the same needles, cast on 24 stitches and knit until you reach the desired length or until you run out of yarn, whichever comes first.

Never be lacking in zeal, but keep your spiritual fervor, serving the Lord.

Romans 12:11

Dear Lord, thank You for the men and women who keep us safe in parking lots and as children walk to and from school. I ask You to put a shield of protection around them. Keep them safe. I ask that when they wear this hat on those cold and chilly days, they will remember Your love and protection for them. It is in the name of Jesus that I pray these things. Amen.

SLOUCHY SEED STITCH HAT

Do you know a busy young mom who is doing well if she is able to brush her hair in the morning? That mom used to be me.

My morning outfit was sweats and a ball cap. Some days I even drove the kids to school in my pajamas and house slippers, praying the whole time I wouldn't have to get out of my car for something. Had I then been capable of knitting more than scarves and baby hats, I would have been wearing a cute hat like this rather than a ball cap!

In fact, all of us busy moms are in this together! Too many women beat themselves up because they aren't the "perfect" mom. Trust me, I've had plenty of mommy guilt. Like the time I forgot to send my son a turkey sandwich for his first grade Thanksgiving feast. I remembered to send the pumpkin bread dessert for the class. But I missed the part of the letter that said to send a sandwich for my own child.

None of us are always going to get it right, but thankfully, through the grace of Jesus, we are all given a clean and new slate every day. By giving this hat to a young mom you may see at the carpool, she will know she is not alone.

SKILL LEVEL ♡♡

MATERIALS

Size US 13 (9 mm) 16-inch circular needle

1 skein bulky/super bulky red yarn for the ribbing and pom-pom*

Approximately 77 yards of bulky/super bulky yarn, for the main color*

Stitch marker

Row counter

Small pom-pom maker

I used Bernat Softee Chunky for both colors of yarn.

DIRECTIONS

With red yarn, CO 44 stitches.

Rnds 1-5: *K2P2*; PM at end of first rnd. (Be careful to not twist that first rnd when joining in the rnd.)

Rnd 6: Switch to MC. *K8, M1*, ending with K4. (49 stitches)

Rnd 7: *K1P1*. (This begins the seed stitch pattern, which is worked over an odd number of stitches, so that you K on the P stitches and P on the K stitches to create the bumpy effect.)

Continue in seed stitch until your piece measures 8½ to 9 inches from the beginning (longer if you want the hat really slouchy).

Once your piece is the desired length, begin decrease as follows:

Make sure you are on a rnd that the first stitch is a P (meaning that you will K the first stitch).

Decrease Rnd 1: *K1, P3tog*, ending with K1. (25 stitches)

Decrease Rnd 2: *P3tog, K1*, ending with P1. (13 stitches)

CARE INSTRUCTIONS

Machine wash in cold water, delicate cycle; air dry or tumble dry, low heat.

Leaving a long tail, cut yarn and pull through the remaining stitches. Cinch yarn tight and sew up the top portion so that it doesn't come undone.

Make a small red pom-pom for the top. Attach pom-pom and weave in ends. Attach a gift tag.

God saved us and called us to live a holy life. He did this, not because we deserved it, but because that was his plan from before the beginning of time—to show us his grace through Christ Jesus.

2 Timothy 1:9 NLT

Dear Lord, I pray for the young mother who will receive this hat. Help her release feelings of guilt when she is led to believe she has failed as a mother. I ask that she will believe that Your grace and mercy are bigger than any of her inadequacies. I ask that You bless her with some extra time this week to take care of her needs in addition to caring for others. It is in the name of Jesus that I pray these things. Amen.

EAR WARMER/HEADBAND

Sometimes it is hard to hear God's voice when so many other messages are bombarding us. We've all experienced moments when we struggled to discern God's leading, when it's hard to sort out the message the world is telling us from the words the Lord is speaking to us.

Perhaps you know someone who just graduated from high school or college who is feeling this way. Or you're familiar with someone considering a career change or wrestling with whether she should be a stay-at-home mom.

When you give the individual this headband, let her know you are praying for God to open her ears to hear His voice for His will in her life. God has a plan for her, and sometimes it takes another person speaking out to remind her that, as a child of God, she has the ability to discern the voice of her personal Shepherd.

SKILL LEVEL ♡ ♡

MATERIALS

Size US 13 (9mm) 16-inch circular needle

Super bulky or bulky yarn, 1 skein each in red and your choice for main color*

I used Lion Brand Hometown USA for both of my colors.

CARE INSTRUCTIONS

Machine wash in cool water, delicate cycle; tumble dry on low or air dry.

DIRECTIONS

With red yarn, CO 50 stitches.

Rnd 1: Switch to MC. Join in the rnd, being careful not to twist the stitches; K.

Rnds 2-3: P.

Rnds 4-5: K.

Rnds 6-7: P.

Rnds 8-9: K.

Rnds 10-11: P.

Rnd 12: Switch to red yarn; K.

BO. Weave in ends. Attach a gift tag.

My sheep listen to my voice; I know them, and they follow me.

John 10:27

Dear Lord, I pray that the woman who receives this headband will be able to discern Your voice and Your will for her life. I ask that You mute any voices that will lead her away from Your grand plan for her. Continue to open her ears to hear the voice of her mighty Shepherd. It is in the name of Jesus that I pray these things. Amen.

Baby Gifts

Baby/Stroller Blanket
34

Baby Hat with Topknot and Matching Mitts
38

Striped Baby Bib
42

Baby Booties
46

BABY/STROLLER BLANKET

Whenever I give these baby blankets made out of blanket yarn, I'm told how soft they are and how much the family likes them. So much so that I often receive requests for an adult version of them! I made a baby blanket out of this yarn for my niece's daughter three years ago. The yarn is super soft, and she still uses the blanket today. In fact, her dad teases her and asks her if he can have her blanket because he wants one of his own.

This is the perfect gift to bring for your first visit with the new parents and baby. It could also be given at a baby shower. Whenever you decide to bless the family with one or both versions of this blanket, let them know how you have been praying for this child before they were even born.

You can make the smaller size to use with the stroller or car seat, but if you are willing to spend a little more time on this, the larger size will get more use. By the way, I used size 15 needles, so it knits up quickly. The larger one took me about 12 hours and the smaller one only 4 hours.

SKILL LEVEL

MATERIALS

Size US 15 (10 mm) 36- to 40-inch circular needle

1 skein bulky red yarn, such as Bernat Blanket Yarn (220 yards in one skein)*

2 skeins your choice for main color yarn*

Stitch marker

You could use 3 skeins of self-striping or variegated yarn for the entire project. I used Bernat Blanket yarn.

CARE INSTRUCTIONS

Machine wash in cool or warm water; tumble dry on low.

DIRECTIONS

For the larger version of this blanket, using red yarn, CO 90 stitches (CO 50 for the smaller stroller blanket).

Rows 1-3: K.

Row 4: Switch to MC yarn (or simply continue using the striped or variegated yarn); K (RS). (You can place a marker to denote the RS.)

Row 5: K3, P to last 3 stitches, K3 (WS).

Repeat rows 4 and 5 until about 1 inch short of desired length is reached. (See note at end of instructions for lengths.) When you are on the WS of the piece (the purl side), still using your MC, knit across the row.

For your next row (RS), switch to the red yarn. Your last 4 rows will be as follows:

Row 1: K.

Row 2: P3, K to last 3 stitches, P3.

Row 3: K.

Row 4: P3, K to last 3 stitches, P3.

BO. Weave in ends. Attach a gift tag.

My larger blanket was 36 x 52 inches, but you can knit it whatever length you would like. The stroller blanket was 22 x 30 inches, which is the standard size for that blanket, so you want to keep as close to that size as possible. If you are up for making both the larger and smaller blanket, you'll need 4 skeins of this blanket yarn.

Children are a gift from the Lord; they are a reward from him.

Psalm 127:3 NLT

Dear Lord, as I knit this blanket, I pray for a healthy baby and a smooth delivery. I know that this child is a reward from You, whether biological or adopted. I pray for the parents to be reminded when they use this gift that their child is wrapped in the loving arms of Jesus. I ask for this child to have a heart for You. It is in the name of Jesus that I pray these things. Amen.

BABY HAT WITH TOPKNOT AND MATCHING MITTS

*I*s someone in your life pregnant or adopting? This basic knit baby hat with matching mitts would be the perfect handmade gift for them! If the individual is someone close to you, this is a sweet addition to include in a baby shower gift. However, the person could be someone you don't know very well, but God has laid it on your heart to bless her with some kind of a hand-knit baby item. For instance, the first time I made this hat, I made two of them. My pharmacy tech was expecting twins—a boy and a girl!

The second time, I gave this gift to an employee at a grocery store I frequent weekly. When the woman checked me out and I realized she was expecting, I asked if she knew if she was having a boy or girl. She told me she was having a girl, and I knew I wanted to bless her with a baby hat with a red bow that would be precious on her sweet infant.

SKILL LEVEL ♡♡♡

MATERIALS

Size US 8 (5 mm) 8-inch circular needle

4 Size US 8 (5 mm) double-pointed needles

Stitch marker

Yarn needle (for optional bow)

Cotton or cotton/acrylic blend* worsted weight yarn, your color choice

Cotton or cotton/acrylic blend* worsted weight yarn, red

The yarn featured in the photo is Hobby Lobby's I Love This Cotton.

CARE INSTRUCTIONS

Machine wash in cold water; lay flat to dry.

DIRECTIONS

BABY HAT WITH TOPKNOT

With the red yarn and circular needle, CO 60 stitches.

Rnds 1-6: K2P2. Be careful to not twist that first rnd when joining in the rnd. PM when you finish your first rnd.

Rnd 7: Switch to MC and K until piece measures 4 inches from the beginning.

For decrease

You will need to switch to your double-pointed needles once it gets too hard to knit your stitches; divide stitches equally on 3 needles.

Rnd 1: *K5, SSK*, ending with K4. (52 stitches)

Rnd 2: K.

Rnd 3: *K4, SSK *, ending with K4. (44 stitches)

Rnd 4: K.

Rnd 5: *K3, SSK*, ending with K4. (36 stitches)

Rnd 6: K. (This is where I switched to my double-pointed needles.)

Rnd 7: *K2, SSK*. (27 stitches)

Rnd 8: K.

Rnd 9: *K1, SSK*. (18 stitches)

Rnd 10: K.

Rnd 11: SSK. (9 stitches)

Rnd 12: Switch to the red yarn; K. (Switching to your red yarn is a bit tricky, so you need to make sure you tie the red yarn to your MC yarn.)

Rnd 13: SSK until 5 stitches remain. (If making a pom-pom for the top, cut an 8-inch tail and pull through these last 5 stitches.)

With these last 5 stitches, K a 4-inch I-cord for the topknot. You will use two double-pointed needles to make your I-cord. ◼◀ Once the I-cord is 4 inches in length, cut the yarn and pull it through the 5 stitches and cinch. Weave in ends.

Optional Bow: If I know the baby is going to be a girl, I like to make a small bow to put on the hat. To make a bow, CO 12 stitches using the red yarn. Knit in garter stitch (knitting every row) for 3 inches. BO; tightly wrap MC yarn around the center to make the bow. Use the yarn needle and a bit of matching yarn or thread to attach the bow to the hat. I have also crocheted with the MC around the edges of the bow for contrast and glued a rhinestone in the center.

BABY MITTS

Using double-pointed needles with red yarn, CO 20 stitches. Place 7 stitches each on needles 1 and 2, and 6 stitches on needle 3. Join to work in the rnd, being careful to not twist your stitches.

Rnds 1-6: K2P2; PM on your first stitch.

Rnds 7-17: Switch to MC; K.

Rnd 18: Switch to red yarn; K.

Rnd 19: *K2, SSK*; repeat to end of rnd. (15 stitches)

Rnds 20-21: K.

Rnd 22: *K1, SSK*; repeat to end of rnd. (10 stitches)

Rnd 23: SSK. (5 stitches)

Cut the yarn and thread it through the yarn needle. Pull the stitches through the remaining 5 stitches. Pull tight to close up the hole. Turn inside out and make a few stitches to make sure the hole stays closed. Weave in ends.

Repeat directions for second baby mitt.

Tuck your baby mitts inside of the hat. Attach the gift tag to the hat.

He took the children in his arms, placed his hands on them and blessed them.

Mark 10:16

Dear Lord, I know that Your hand is on this baby and that You will bless him or her. I pray for a healthy baby and pregnancy for this mother. Let her delivery be free from complications. I pray that if this mother does not know You, this gift will be a seed of faith planted in her life. For the woman who does believe in Jesus, I pray that she continues to trust You and Your perfect ways for this baby's life. It is in the name of Jesus that I pray these things. Amen.

STRIPED BABY BIB

When I started creating the pattern for this bib, I was on a flight to New York. It usually takes me one or two pattern attempts to make the pattern just right. Due to flight delays, I was able to almost finish two of these bibs. (Part of the reason I knit a second bib was that my first one was solid blue and red. I thought I'd prefer to picture a striped one here.)

The next morning, while eating breakfast at our hotel, I noticed our server was expecting. After we finished our meal, I asked her due date and if she knew the gender of her baby. I told her I liked to knit and had just made a baby bib I would like to give to her. When she told me she was having a boy, I had no doubt God wanted me to give her the first bib. Our waitress had beautiful blue eyes—similar to the color of the bib's yarn. As I gave it to her, I told her, "If your baby has your same beautiful blue eyes, this bib is going to match them." I included a card with Psalm 139 written on it and let her know I liked to give gifts to people who had made a difference in my day and I appreciated her kindness to us. I also let her know I would be praying for a healthy baby and a smooth delivery for her.

Is someone expecting at one of the businesses you frequent? Or is there someone else on your heart who would love this cute bib for her baby? Step out in faith and give her this handmade gift that shows God's love for her and her precious baby.

SKILL LEVEL ♡ ♡

MATERIALS

Size US 7 (4.5mm) straight needles

1 skein cotton or cotton blend yarn, red*

1 skein cotton or cotton blend yarn, your choice for main color*

Stitch holder

Stitch marker (optional)

Row counter

Sew-on snap (I used size 4.)

Thread and needle for snap

I used Cascade Sarasota yarn, which is a cotton acrylic blend.

DIRECTIONS

This bib is an infant-sized bib, so depending on what yarn you use, you can get multiple bibs out of your 2 skeins of yarn, or you can make the basic knit baby hat pattern to accompany it.

With red yarn, CO 28 stitches.

Rows 1-3: K.

Row 4: K3, P to last 3 stitches, K3.

Row 5: K. (If you want to place a stitch marker on this side as a reminder that this is the RS of the piece, you can do that.)

Row 6: K3, P to last 3 stitches, K3.

Every 6 rows you will switch colors.

As you continue to knit, switch yarn color as follows:

Row 12: Change yarn color.

Row 18: Change yarn color.

Row 24: Change yarn color.

CARE INSTRUCTIONS

Machine wash in cool or warm water; tumble dry on low or medium heat.

Row 30: Change yarn color.

Row 36: Change yarn color.

Row 44 will be in red.

Your odd rows will be K rows (RS) and your even rows will be K3, P to last 3 stitches, K3.

Row 37: K.

Row 38: K3, P to last 3 stitches, K3.

Row 39: K.

Row 40: K3, P to last 3 stitches, K3.

Rows 41-43: K.

Row 44 will start your BO. Slip the first 6 stitches onto a stitch holder. Using a new piece of yarn, BO the last 22 stitches. Slip the 6 stitches back on your needle and K 53 rows. BO for row 54. If using a snap, sew onto the neck and bib portion. You can also use a small piece of sew-on Velcro. The width of my bib was 5½ inches x 6 inches. Attach a gift tag.

You created my inmost being; you knit me together in my mother's womb.

Psalm 139:13

Dear Lord, while I may only casually know the recipient of this gift, I pray for a healthy baby, pregnancy, and delivery. I ask that the baby's mother not only believes that the baby inside of her has been knit by You in her womb, but also that she knows that You have fearfully and wonderfully made her as well. It is in the name of Jesus that I pray these things. Amen.

BABY BOOTIES

Do you know of a baby who is going to be born into a Christian household? The red on the sole of these booties is a symbol of God being this child's foundation. This color also serves as a reminder to the parent each time they slip these booties over those cute little toes that this baby is a child of the King.

If the parents don't share your faith, maybe the grandparents do. In that case, these booties can be given to the grandparents to give to their grandchild. Christian grandparents have a unique opportunity to pray for and to be godly mentors to their grandchildren. This is especially true when grandparents assist with their grandchild's care.

The red color on booties is a cute and creative way to remind the parents or grandparents how important it is to make sure this baby has Jesus as his or her foundation.

SKILL LEVEL ♡ ♡ ♡

MATERIALS

Size US 7 (4.5 mm) straight needles

Worsted weight yarn, red

Worsted weight yarn, your choice for main color

Yarn needle

CARE INSTRUCTIONS

Hand-wash in cool water or machine wash in cold water, delicate cycle; tumble dry on low or air dry.

DIRECTIONS

Using red yarn, CO 24 stitches, leaving a 6-inch tail. You will do a K1P1 ribbing for the first part of this pattern. ■◀

Rows 1-10: With red yarn, *K1P1*; repeat to end.

Row 11: Switch to MC yarn, K. Mark as RS. (Leave a 6-inch tail of MC, so you can use it to sew up the sides.)

Rows 12-19: *K1P1*; repeat to end.

Row 20: CO 6 stitches. ■◀ You will K these 6 stitches and the 24 stitches on the needle. Once you have K all 30 stitches, CO 6 more stitches. When you are knitting the 6 new CO stitches, make sure you pull that last stitch tight, so you don't have a hole between your last CO stitch and your original 24 stitches. You will now have a total of 36 stitches for the remaining rows.

Rows 21-30: K.

Rows 31-34: Switch to red yarn. (This should be the RS of the piece when you make the color change.)

Row 35: BO, leaving a 12-inch tail to sew up the sole of the bootie.

Fold the right sides of the piece together—the wrong side of the piece will be facing toward the outside. To sew up the toe, pull the yarn to the outside stitch on each side of the toe and pull to cinch it to form the toe portion. Sew up the sides and bottom, and then turn piece right side out. Attach a gift tag.

Anyone who listens to my teaching and follows it is wise, like a person who builds a house on solid rock.

Matthew 7:24 NLT

Dear Lord, I pray for this baby to be raised on Your firm foundation. No matter what comes his or her way, You are the Rock. With You, this child will not crumble or fall. I ask that You draw this baby's family closer to You. If the grandparents are involved, I ask that You give them opportunities to share Jesus with both their own children and this new grandbaby. It is in the name of Jesus that I pray these things. Amen.

Bags and Totes

Felted Book Bag
50

Felted Gift
Card Holder
54

Felted Reading
Glasses Case
56

Beach Bag
58

Felted Book Bag

Do you know of someone who has decided to go back to school later in life to either start, finish, or pursue an advanced degree? Maybe there is a high school or college student in your life who would appreciate the gift of this felted book bag.

As I typed this pattern, I thought of a woman in her late 40s who recently stepped out in boldness to pursue a degree. As a single mom, she had temporarily put some of her dreams on the back burner. I plan on giving her this bag along with some spiral notebooks, pens, and pencils, as well as an encouraging note.

If you are giving this gift to a high school or college student, let them know how proud you are that they are putting their education first.

SKILL LEVEL ♡ ♡ ♡

MATERIALS

Size US 10½ (10.5 mm) 24-inch circular needle

Stitch marker

4 stitch holders (for handles)

Row counter

Yarn needle

1½ skeins 100% wool worsted weight yarn, red (210 yards in each skein)*

2 to 3 skeins (approximately 327 yards total) 100% wool worsted weight yarn, your color choice*

*I used 2 skeins of Patons Classic Wool for the red yarn and 3 skeins of Noro Kureyon for the MC.

DIRECTIONS

BOOK BAG

To knit the bottom/base of the bag, with red yarn CO 50 stitches. Work in garter stitch (K every row) for 50 rnds.

This next part is a bit tricky because you will be picking up stitches on the other three sides of the base of the bag but won't be picking up every stitch. Without turning your work, pick up and K17 stitches, evenly spacing the stitches as best as you can, on the next (short) side. Pick up and K50 stitches on the next (long) side. Finally, pick up and K17 stitches on the last (short) side, evenly spacing the stitches as best as you can. PM to mark the beginning of the rnd. You should have a total of 134 stitches. ▪️

Being careful to not twist your stitches, begin knitting in the rnd, which will produce the stockinette stitch. Knit 4 rnds in red and then switch to MC beginning with the fifth rnd.

Continue to K in MC until the piece measures 16 inches from the bottom of the bag.

Switch back to red and K for 5 rnds. The sixth rnd will start the handles.

HANDLES

K11 and place these stitches on a stitch holder.

BO 29 stitches.

K11 and place these stitches on a stitch holder. (Your last BO stitch is considered your first K stitch, so you are really knitting 10 stitches.)

Note: A friend who is a loose knitter tried this pattern, and her bag ended up much larger. If you are a loose knitter and would like a smaller bag, go down to a size 9 or 10 needle.

CARE INSTRUCTIONS

Hand-wash in cold water; air dry.

BO 16 stitches. (This is the short side of your bag.)

K11 and place stitches on a stitch holder. (Again, the first stitch of your K11 is your last BO stitch.) BO 29 stitches.

K11 and place on a stitch holder. BO 16 stitches (the other short side). At this point, there should be 16 stitches left on your needle.

BO the final 16 stitches; there will be one stitch remaining on the needle. Cut yarn, leaving a tail, and pull it through the last stitch. Weave in that end.

Place 11 stitches from the first stitch holder on a knitting needle and attach a double strand of the red yarn. Work the doubled yarn in stockinette stitch (K one row, P one row) until it measures 35 inches. (Stockinette stitch causes the handle to roll on the sides, which I didn't think I liked. So I had a friend make a bag with the handles K in garter stitch, but I liked the stockinette one better. The garter stitch does lie flat, but it won't felt up as nicely, so if you choose to use garter stitch for the handles, you'll need to make the handles a bit shorter.)

After you have completed 35 inches, cut a 12- to 16-inch tail for joining your stitches from needle 1 to needle 2. To do this, you can graft the stitches from your first needle to the stitches on the second stitch holder using the Kitchener stitch, which looks the best. However, because you are going to felt the bag, this join won't really show, so you can always *loosely* stitch them together instead. ◾️

For the second handle, repeat what you did for the first handle. Place the 11 stitches from the third stitch holder on your needle and K until the handle measures 35 inches in length. Graft the handle stitches onto the stitches from the fourth stitch holder. Sew in all loose ends.

You are now ready to felt! Follow the felting instructions on page 11. When felting is complete, stuff with plastic grocery bags or rags to help the bag hold its shape; hang to dry. Attach a gift tag.

Note: The body of my bag unfelted was 17 inches high and 17 inches wide. After I felted the bag, it was approximately 12 inches high and 14 inches wide.

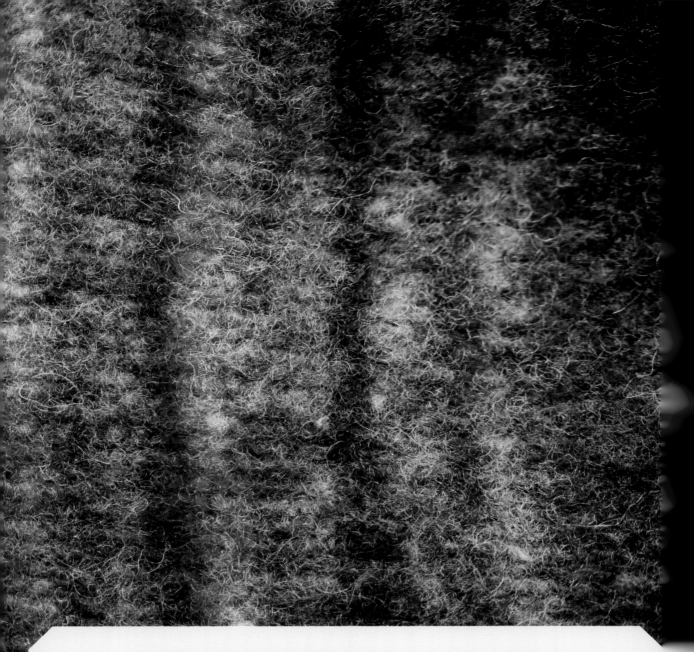

Search for the LORD and for his strength; continually seek him.

1 Chronicles 16:11 NLT

Dear Lord, I pray that the person who receives this bag will not feel overwhelmed with all of her assignments and exams. I pray for retention and recollection when she is taking tests and writing essays. I ask for perseverance when she doesn't get the grade she expected. Give her boldness and courage to talk to her professors when she needs help or guidance. It is in the name of Jesus that I pray these things. Amen.

FELTED GIFT CARD HOLDER

Sometimes a day of pampering spent with a girlfriend is all someone needs to boost her self-confidence. Can you think of a friend or relative who could use a little attention to feel prettier? Something as simple as a date to get a manicure or pedicure is all it takes. You can place a gift card to a nail salon in this felted gift card holder along with a note that you will book the appointments for the two of you to go together.

This little gift card holder is also the perfect size for a pocket mirror. I found a small, rectangular mirror online and glued the Scripture part of the tag to the back of it. This way every time my friend uses the mirror, she is reminded of how God has fearfully and wonderfully made her.

SKILL LEVEL ♡ ♡

MATERIALS

Size US 9 (5.5 mm) straight needles

100% wool worsted weight yarn, red

100% wool worsted weight yarn, coordinating color

Row counter

Size 1 sew-on snaps

Needle and thread

CARE INSTRUCTIONS

Hand-wash in cold water; air dry.

DIRECTIONS

With the red yarn, CO 2 stitches.

Row 1: K.

Rows 2-19: In the first stitch of every row, KFB and then K the rest of the stitches, so you will increase one stitch on every row (20 stitches after row 19).

Rows 20-43: (Mark row 20 as RS of the piece.) Switch to MC and K all rows.

Rows 44-49: Switch back to red yarn and K all rows.

Rows 50-67: Switch back to MC and K all rows.

BO and weave in ends.

Sew up the sides; fold the point over the top. You are now ready to felt it. (See felting instructions on page 11.) When you reach the desired size after felting, allow the gift card holder to air dry and then sew part of your snap to the underside of the point and match the bottom part of the snap with it and sew to the body of your item. You can also use permanent bond Velcro if you prefer. Before felting, mine was 4½ x 4½ inches. After felting it was 3½ inches wide and 2½ inches tall with the top folded down.

Add a gift card and gift tag inside the holder.

I praise you because I am fearfully and wonderfully made; your works are wonderful…

Psalm 139:14

Dear Lord, I pray that my friend finds her confidence in You. When she looks in the mirror, lift her up so she sees her beauty as You see it. You knew exactly what You were doing when You created her in her mother's womb. I ask that she be infused with a spirit that radiates the beauty within her. It is in the name of Jesus that I pray these things. Amen.

Felted Reading Glasses Case

Do you have a mentor in your life who has guided you or even stepped in as a parent or grandparent figure? Maybe you live in an area where you are not in close proximity to your immediate family or possibly you are estranged from them. Whatever the case, you can be grateful for a person in your life whom you go to for guidance, wisdom, or help in your spiritual growth.

If your mentor uses reading glasses, this gift would be the perfect accessory for him or her. Now even the dollar stores carry "readers," but often they don't come with a case. The cases you can purchase are not nearly as cute as this one, nor are they made with the same love and prayers.

If you know the strength of your mentor's reading glasses, you can even pick up an extra pair to give with this gift. Take it from me: One can never have too many pairs of reading glasses! When you give this gift to the recipient, make sure you let them know how much their kindness, love, and encouragement has impacted your life.

SKILL LEVEL ♡ ♡

MATERIALS

4 size US 10 (6 mm) double-pointed needles

100% wool worsted weight yarn, your choice for the main color

100% wool worsted weight yarn, red

Row counter

CARE INSTRUCTIONS

Hand-wash in cold water; air dry.

DIRECTIONS

Using 3 needles and red yarn, CO 24 stitches; divide stitches evenly between the 3 needles. The fourth needle will be your working needle.

Rnds 1-4: K.

Rnds 5-35: Switch to MC and K all rnds.

Rnds 36-39: Switch to red yarn and K all rnds.

Divide the stitches evenly between 2 needles; turn your piece inside out and BO using the 3-needle BO. ◼

You are now ready to felt your project. See page 11 for felting instructions. My piece was approximately 6 inches x 2½ inches before felting. Use a safety pin to attach your gift tag.

Let each generation tell its children of your mighty acts; let them proclaim your power.

Psalm 145:4 NLT

Dear Lord, I thank You for providing mentors in my life to guide me spiritually. I praise You for the guidance and wisdom that my mentors have invested in me. I ask that You continue to bless them with the gift to point others to Jesus. It is in the name of Jesus that I pray these things. Amen.

BEACH BAG

When my mother-in-law resided in an assisted living facility, the activity director, who put in many hours of hard work every week, took a well-deserved weeklong cruise. At the time, I didn't have this beach bag pattern complete, but I did buy her a bag and filled it with things she could use on her trip.

I can think of so many people like this activity director who have a hard time getting away from their jobs to make time for themselves. According to Scripture, even Jesus knew that His disciples were growing weary and needed rest. Jesus desires for us to do the same. Can you think of someone who is going on—or is in need of—a long-overdue vacation? You can give her this much-appreciated gift to aid in her relaxation.

This bag doesn't have to be specifically for a beach vacation. It could be given as a "staycation" gift and filled with sunscreen, a favorite book, or whatever else you would like to include to encourage a relaxing day or weekend. The purpose of this gift is to invite the person to take the time for a day of rest. If you have a pool or belong to a club that has one, maybe you can even request that she join you there for a laid-back afternoon.

SKILL LEVEL ♡ ♡ ♡ ♡

MATERIALS

Size US 8 (5 mm) 24-inch circular needle

1 to 2 skeins (200 yards) cotton red yarn*

2 skeins (200 yards) cotton yarn, your choice for the main color*

Stitch marker

Yarn needle (to sew handles) or size US 8 double-pointed needles if you prefer the 3-needle bind off

Cable stitch holder

Row counter

I used Hobby Lobby's Crafter's Choice yarn. You will double the red yarn for the bottom of the bag, so if you don't want to pull the yarn from the center and outside of one skein to double, use 2 skeins.

DIRECTIONS

BEACH BAG

With 2 strands of red yarn, CO 44 stitches.

K for 34 rows. At the end of Row 34, do not turn your work. Rotate it and pick up 14 stitches along the short side of the base, then pick up 44 stitches on the long side and 14 stitches more on the other short side. ◼◀ You should have a total of 116 stitches now. PM for beginning of the rnd. Cut the yarn and tie down to anchor to your piece before you K your first rnd.

You will now be working in the rnd. Being careful to not twist your stitches, start knitting your first rnd with one strand of the red yarn. The first rnd may be a little tricky to K from the picked-up stitches. K 3 rows in red; switch to MC.

K 4 rnds before starting the lace pattern.

You will start the lace pattern below on the fifth rnd. Because this is a lace pattern, you may want to use a lifeline on one of your K rows, moving it periodically. ◼◀

LACE PATTERN

(I use a small sticky note and move it after each row so I don't lose my place.)

Rnd 1: *YO, K2tog*; repeat to end of rnd.

Rnd 2: K.

Rnd 3: *YO, SSK*; repeat to end of rnd.

Rnd 4: K.

Work this lace pattern until the piece measures approximately 11 inches. You will now start the handle directions below.

HANDLES

BO 14 stitches; K44 and slip these stitches onto a cable stitch holder. BO 14 stitches; K44 (the first of the K44 stitches is already on your right needle). Each handle will be 44 stitches, which you will work flat and then join together when you are done with both of them. Cut yarn. Because you will be starting the handles on the right side of the piece, you will be adding new yarn for each of the handles for the first row.

Row 1: (RS) K2tog, *YO, K2tog* to last 2 stitches, K2tog. (42 stitches)

Row 2: (WS) P.

Row 3: K1, SSK, *YO, SSK* to last 3 stitches, SSK, K1. (40 stitches)

Row 4: P.

Row 5: K1, K2tog, *YO, K2tog* to last 3 stitches, K2tog, K1. (38 stitches)

Row 6: P.

Row 7: SSK, *YO, SSK* to last 2 stitches, SSK. (36 stitches)

Row 8: P.

Repeat rows 5-8 until you have 20 stitches after you complete row 8. (You will continue to decrease 2 stitches on your odd rows as you have been.).

When you have 20 stitches, switch to red yarn. Continue repeating rows 5-8 until 8 stitches remain, ending with an 8-stitch P row (row 8).

Work the remaining 8 stitches with these 4 rows:

Row 1: (RS): K1, *YO, K2tog* 3 times, K1.

Row 2: P.

Row 3: K1, *YO, SSK* 3 times, K1.

Row 4: P.

At this point you can cut the yarn, leaving about an 8-inch tail and move the remaining 8 stitches onto a cable stitch holder so you can do a 3-needle BO after you complete the other handle. ◼◣

If you don't want to do the 3-needle BO, at this point, you can loosely BO the stitches and sew the two ends together once you have finished the second handle. For a stronger handle, I prefer the 3-needle BO.

Move the remaining 44 stitches off the cable stitch holder to your needles and repeat the above sequence for the second handle.

FINISHING

Either use a large needle to sew the ends of the two handles together or use the 3-needle BO (turn your piece inside out for the 3-needle BO). Weave in ends and put whatever gifts you would like to include in the bag. Attach a gift tag.

Because so many people were coming and going that they did not even have a chance to eat, he said to them, "Come with me by yourselves to a quiet place and get some rest."

Mark 6:31

Dear Lord, I ask that You bless this woman's job and also allow her to take some time to find rest for her soul. Please give her quiet time that will renew her spirit. Fill her up so that she can be recharged when she returns to work. It is in the name of Jesus that I pray these things. Amen.

Pets

Cat Toy
64

Spool Knit
Felted Dog Leash
68

Pet
Bandanna
70

CAT TOY

Due to my cat allergy and an aversion to cleaning a litter box, I am not a cat person. However, I know plenty of people who are. They would even argue that having a cat is better than having a dog.

Because I am not a cat person, I had to go to a good friend and fellow knitter, Patti, to not only design this pattern, but to also share with me why she liked having a cat. Patti told me that, like dogs, cats bring much devotion, love, and comfort to their owners.

Can you think of a cat lover in your life who would appreciate your thoughtfulness in recognizing her love for her feline companion? Not only will this cute little cat toy with a floppy tail and bell keep her cat entertained, but it will also bring smiles to the owner's face when she sees her kitty playing with it. Along with the toy, you can include some catnip to be enjoyed as well.

SKILL LEVEL ♡ ♡ ♡

MATERIALS

4 size US 8 (5 mm) double-pointed needles

Worsted weight yarn, red

Worsted weight yarn, your choice for main color

Stitch marker

Row counter

Polyester fiberfill stuffing

3/16-inch x 12-inch wooden dowel

Yarn needle

Jingle bell

CARE INSTRUCTIONS

Hand-wash in cool or warm water; air dry.

DIRECTIONS

With red yarn CO 3 stitches. K an I-cord with the red yarn for 6 inches for the tail.

Divide 3 stitches onto 3 needles (1 stitch on each needle).

Switch to MC. Tie MC to the red yarn to anchor it.

KFB in each stitch until you have 21 stitches total. This should be 6 rnds. Place your stitch marker on the yarn on needle 1.

Rnds 1-12: K.

(For Rnds 13-14, you will be making the ears.)

Rnd 13: On needle 1, KFBF, *K*, KFBF last stitch. K all stitches on needles 2-3.

Rnd 14: On needle 1, K3tog, *K*, K3tog last stitch. K all stitches on needles 2-3.

For decrease

Rnds 15-18: On each needle, K2tog twice, and then K to end of needle (you will be decreasing 3 stitches on each rnd). You should have 6 stitches on your needles.

Stuff the toy with the polyester fiberfill until your mouse takes shape.

Rnd 19: Switch to red yarn; K2tog on the first stitch of each needle until you have 3 stitches left (2 rnds). Cut an 8- to 10-inch tail, thread through your yarn needle, and pull through those 3 stitches; tie a knot to anchor it. Tie the remainder of this yarn piece to your wooden dowel. You can put a dab of glue to hold it in place or let it slide up and down as you use it to play with the cat. Attach the jingle bell to the mouse's tail, along with your gift tag.

Every animal of the forest is mine, and the cattle on a thousand hills. I know every bird in the mountains, and the insects in the fields are mine. If I were hungry I would not tell you, for the world is mine, and all that is in it.

Isaiah 58:7 NLT

Dear Lord, thank You that You provide us with animals that can bring us unconditional love and affection. I ask that this cat will continue to bring its owner comfort and companionship throughout the day. If her day has been frustrating, let her cat's playtime bring a smile to her face and be a reminder of how You love and provide for her on a daily basis. It is in the name of Jesus that I pray these things. Amen.

Spool Knit
Felted Dog Leash

A woman in my neighborhood walks her little dog every day. I love watching them together. I think it would be fun to make her one of these dog leashes. With all of the dog-friendly places popping up these days, there should be plenty of opportunities for you to give away this super easy dog leash.

Do you visit a coffee shop on a regular basis where you consistently see the same family with their dog on the patio? Or are there people in your neighborhood whom you routinely see walking their dogs? Gifting a dog owner with this felted leash is an easy way to step out in faith and let someone know you notice them and their furry best friend. And it's a great way to share the love of Jesus.

An I-cord is something that can be made using double-pointed needles, but for a project like this, using a spool knitter is easier. Even someone who doesn't know how to knit or crochet may find this to be the perfect introduction to a knitting project.

SKILL LEVEL ♡

MATERIALS

Jumbo spool knitter (8 pegs)

Loom hook

Yarn needle

Trigger snap or swivel hook

1 skein or scraps of 100% wool worsted weight yarn

1 skein 100% wool worsted weight yarn, red

CARE INSTRUCTIONS

Machine wash on delicate cycle or hand-wash in cold water; air dry.

DIRECTIONS

This leash can be made using one strand or double strands of yarn. For a thicker leash, you will need to use double strands. The striped leash in the photo was made using one strand. For a thicker leash, use double strands.

Using your jumbo spool knitter, start your project with the red wool yarn. This will be the handle for your leash. You will make this portion approximately 14 inches long. You can either make your leash in one solid color or alternate colors using whatever 100% wool scrap yarn you have. For my striped one, I used 3 different colors and switched colors when I could see the yarn coming out of the bottom of the spool, which ended up being about 4 inches.

When your piece measures approximately 86 inches, switch to the red yarn for the last 4 inches. Your unfelted piece will be around 90 inches long. BO using the basic BO in the rnd for the loom. ■ You will thread this end through your trigger snap and sew it down to anchor it. Loop the handle portion and sew down the two red ends to make your handle.

It is now ready to felt! Instructions for felting are on page 11. My finished piece was about 72 inches long after felting. For this project, you will need to check more frequently while felting it so your handle doesn't get too small. Attach your gift tag to the trigger snap/swivel hook of the leash.

God created great sea creatures and every living thing that scurries and swarms in the water, and every sort of bird—each producing offspring of the same kind. And God saw that it was good.

Genesis 1:21 NLT

Dear Lord, You created every creature on this earth. You lovingly made each and every one of us. I know that many people consider their dogs their "children" and will appreciate this handmade gift. I ask that whoever receives this gift knows that because You made them, they are good. Lord, I pray that this small gift will be something that draws them to You. It is in the name of Jesus that I pray these things. Amen.

Pet Bandanna

For many people, their dogs are their family. When I made this pattern, a childhood friend who later became my college roommate came to mind. While some people proudly display their children on their annual Christmas cards, she has her dogs professionally photographed for hers.

If you aren't a dog or cat person, it may be difficult to understand the love and attachment someone forms for a pet. This love is unconditional. I can't even describe the loss I felt when we had to euthanize our dog of 15 years. While I loved my dog, I don't really consider myself a dog person. So you can imagine my surprise at the emptiness I felt when he was no longer with us.

Can you think of someone whose "children" are their dogs? Someone who would truly appreciate this gift? This is a super quick project using leftover yarn from a previous project. You could also make the Spool Knit Felted Dog Leash to accompany it.

SKILL LEVEL

MATERIALS

Size US 9 (5.5 mm) straight needles or circular needle

Leftover worsted weight cotton yarn, red*

Leftover worsted weight cotton yarn, your choice for main color*

Row counter

I used Hobby Lobby's I Love This Cotton for both colors of yarn.

CARE INSTRUCTIONS

Machine wash in cool or warm water; tumble dry on low heat.

DIRECTIONS

With red yarn, for the small bandanna CO 50 stitches (medium: 65, large: 80).

Rows 1-4: K.

Row 5 for the small size: BO 15, K19, BO 15. Cut the yarn and pull through the last stitch. (20 stitches left on your needle)

Row 5 for the medium size: BO 20, K24, BO 20. Cut the yarn and pull through the last stitch. (25 stitches left on your needle)

Row 5 for the large size: BO 25, K29, BO 25. Cut the yarn and pull through the last stitch. (30 stitches left on your needle)

(You will now start the stockinette stitch for the triangle portion.)

Row 6: Switch to MC yarn; K.

Row 7: P.

(You will now begin to decrease every other row, which will be on all of the K rows, decreasing on the first and last stitch.)

Row 8: K2tog, K16 (21, 26), K2tog.

Row 9: P.

Row 10: K2tog, K14 (19, 24), K2tog.

Row 11: P.

Row 12: K2tog, K12 (17, 22), K2tog.

Row 13: P.

Row 14: K2tog, K10 (15, 20), K2tog.

Row 15: P.

Row 16: K2tog, K8 (13, 18), K2tog.

Row 17: P.

Row 18: K2tog, K6 (11, 16), K2tog.

Row 19: P.

Row 20: Switch to red yarn for small size only. For medium and large sizes, continue working in MC. K2tog, K4 (9, 14), K2tog.

Row 21: P.

Row 22: K2tog, K2 (7, 12), K2tog.

Row 23: P.

Small

Row 24: K2tog twice.

Row 25: BO; cut yarn and pull through last stitch. Weave in ends.

Medium

Row 24: K2tog, K5, K2tog.

Row 25: P.

Row 26: Switch to red yarn. K2tog, K3, K2tog.

Row 27: P.

Row 28: K2tog, K1, K2tog.

Row 29: P.

Row 30: K2tog, BO, cut yarn and pull through last stitch.

Large

Row 24: K2tog, K10, K2tog.

Row 25: P.

Row 26: K2tog, K8, K2tog.

Row 27: P.

Row 28: K2tog, K6, K2tog.

Row 29: P.

Row 30: Switch to red yarn. K2tog, K4, K2tog

Row 31: P.

Row 32: K2tog, K2, K2tog.

Row 33: P.

Row 34: K2tog twice.

BO; weave in ends. Attach a gift tag.

The godly care for their animals, but the wicked are always cruel.

Proverbs 12:10 NLT

Dear Lord, I praise You that You created animals on this earth. We care for them, and they give us valuable companionship. When the person I make this project for sees this bandanna on their pet, let them also be reminded of Your unconditional love for them. It is in the name of Jesus that I pray these things. Amen.

Scarves

TRIANGLE COMFORT SHAWL

I was 28 when my first husband passed away in an unexpected accident. While I would not have chosen to be a young, pregnant, single mom, because of the comfort I received from my heavenly Father, I am now able to comfort others through my hands, heart, and prayers. I was so moved back then to learn that even strangers were praying for me, and I realized the impact I could have by making prayer shawls to comfort others who are broken and hurting.

These shawls aren't just for those who are grieving. Do you know someone who is suffering from depression, going through a divorce, experiencing the loss of a job, or who maybe recently received an unexpected medical diagnosis and might need a reminder of God's love? This comfort shawl would be perfect for them.

The yarn used for this shawl is what I consider "comfy" yarn. When you wrap yourself in it, you can't help but feel the warmth and love radiating from the one who made it for you. I have given away numerous prayer shawls over the years, the most recent to a newly widowed neighbor. My neighbor told me she will always cherish the shawl I made for her. I have heard similar sentiments from others who have received one as a gift.

SKILL LEVEL ♡♡

MATERIALS

Size US 19 (15 mm) 36-inch (or longer) circular needle

350 yards of bulky yarn, your color choice*

1 skein of bulky yarn, red*

Size P/Q crochet hook

Stitch marker

I used Lion Brand Homespun yarn.

CARE INSTRUCTIONS

If using Homespun yarn, machine wash using the delicate cycle in cold or cool water; lay flat to dry or tumble dry on low heat setting.

DIRECTIONS

With double strands of the red yarn, CO 80 stitches.

Row 1: K.

Row 2: Switch to double strands of MC. K1, K2tog, K to last 3 stitches, K2tog, K1. This will be the RS of your piece. If you are using a stitch marker, you will put a marker on this side of the piece.

Continue Rows 1 and 2 in MC, decreasing stitches every other row (RS rows) until there are 3 stitches left on your needle.

When you have 3 stitches left, cut a 6-inch tail and pull the yarn through those last 3 stitches.

Using two strands of red yarn and your crochet hook, SC 2 rows for edging along the two sides of the triangle. ◼ If you are opposed to crocheting around the edge, you can make a red fringe tassel or pom-pom to put on the point of your triangle. Weave in the ends. Attach a gift tag.

He comforts us in all our troubles so that we can comfort others. When they are troubled, we will be able to give them the same comfort God has given us.

2 Corinthians 1:4 NLT

Dear Lord, I ask that those who receive this shawl will feel Your love and comfort from this gift that was prayed over for them, as well as feel the intercessory prayers that were uttered on their behalf. I pray for these individuals to be drawn closer to You during this difficult time. I know that despite the brokenness they may feel right now, that when they wrap themselves in this shawl they will feel Your loving arms around them. It is in the name of Jesus that I pray these things. Amen.

LOOSE WEAVE
SUMMER SCARF

*I*t's hard to see someone I care about settle for second best. I can't read her mind and understand why she feels that she doesn't deserve God's best for her. It is especially difficult for me to see a friend or family member in an unhealthy relationship. Sometimes I wonder if this person is in a toxic relationship because she thinks she doesn't deserve to be loved. And maybe a handmade gift, along with words, prayers, and support, would help give her the courage to break free and seek God's best.

When you give this gift, ask for the Holy Spirit's words to flow from your mouth. God will give you the right words to say if you go to Him in prayer about this. You can also pray that this scarf will be a reminder of God's love for her and that through Him she can do everything, because Christ will give her the strength.

The color choice on this scarf was intentional. It makes me think of the American flag and the freedom associated with those colors. These colors symbolize the independence this woman will have when she breaks free from the bondage that is keeping her from experiencing the love she deserves.

While this is probably the simplest lace stitch there is, most might not feel the necessity of using a lifeline, but I do. Inevitably, I will make a mistake. Having a lifeline gives me a point to correct without having to start over. Jesus can be our lifeline too. He can heal our broken souls.

SKILL LEVEL ♡ ♡

MATERIALS

Size US 11 (8 mm) straight needles

1 skein worsted weight yarn, red (You only need enough for 3 rows)*

1 skein worsted weight yarn, your choice for main color*

Yarn needle

Stitch marker (optional)

I used Lana Gatto Montecarlo for both colors. (159 yards per skein)

CARE INSTRUCTIONS

Hand-wash in cold water or machine wash, delicate cycle; lay flat to dry.

DIRECTIONS

SCARF

With red yarn CO 20 stitches. K one row. Switch to MC and K second row. (This will be the RS of your piece, so place a stitch marker on this side).

LACE STITCH PATTERN

K4, *YO, K2tog, K2*; repeat between * 4 times, ending with K2.

Repeat this pattern until the desired length. (I knit with my MC until I was near the end of the skein.) At this point, when you are on the WS of the piece, K 1 row with MC, and then switch to red yarn. K 1 row with the red yarn.

BO. Weave in ends. (My scarf was approximately 62 inches in length and 4½ inches wide.) Attach a gift tag.

Note: Because I am prone to make mistakes with any type of lace pattern, I like to use a lifeline, just in case I have to tear out part of my project. 🎥

I can do everything through Christ, who gives me strength.

Philippians 4:13 NLT

Dear Lord, I pray that the person receiving this gift will see her worth in You. I ask that You open her eyes to her present unhealthy view of what love is. Let her see her value as a daughter of the King. When she wraps this scarf around her neck, give her a desire to have a deeper relationship with the only One who can give her unconditional love. It is in the name of Jesus that I pray these things. Amen.

Sonia in Cali
One-Skein Cowl

*M*y sister-in-law, Sonia, serves as the inspiration for this pattern. While visiting her and my brother in California, I was making a cowl that had multiple stitch patterns. She pointed to the row that had a yarn over, knit 2 together pattern and commented that she liked that one the best. This cowl was made with that stitch. I love how it turned out, especially with the variegated yarn.

While Sonia and I were both raised in the church, we really didn't know what it was like to have a strong faith and relationship with Jesus until we were older. When my first husband unexpectedly died, we went on our faith and grief journey together. Over the years, we have both grown spiritually and value not only our friendship, but also our spiritual kinship with one another.

Is there someone in your life who has walked beside you on your spiritual quest, someone you could bless with this gift? This is a way to let her know how much her friendship has meant to you, emotionally and spiritually.

SKILL LEVEL ♡ ♡

MATERIALS

Size US 11 (8mm) 36-inch circular needle

1 skein Ella Rae Seasons or other bulky yarn (219 yards)

Bulky red yarn

Stitch marker

Size J crochet hook

CARE INSTRUCTIONS

Hand-wash or machine wash on the delicate cycle in cold water; lay flat to dry.

DIRECTIONS

CO 100 stitches; PM.

Rnd 1: K. (Be careful to not twist the stitches as you knit this first rnd.)

Rnd 2: P.

Rnd 3: K.

Rnd 4: P.

Rnds 5-8: K.

Rnd 9: P.

Rnd 10: K.

Rnd 11: *YO, K2tog* to end of rnd.

Rnd 12: P.

Rnds 13-16: K.

Rnd 17: P.

Rnd 18: K.

Rnd 19: *YO, K2tog* to end of rnd.

Rnd 20: P.

Rnds 21-24: K.

Rnd 25: P.

Rnd 26: K.

Rnd 27: *YO, K2tog* to end of rnd.

Rnd 28: P.

Rnds 29-32: K.

Rnd 33: P.

Rnd 34: K.

Rnd 35: *YO, K2tog* to end of rnd.

Rnd 36: P.

Rnds 37-40: K.

Rnd 41: P.

Rnd 42: K.

Rnd 43: *YO, K2tog* to end of rnd.

Rnd 44: P.

Rnds 45-48: K.

Rnd 49: P.

Rnd 50: K.

Rnd 51: P.

Rnd 52: K.

BO. Weave in ends. Attach a gift tag.

To add the red crochet chain to weave through the top and bottom of the cowl, chain approximately 80 stitches (or however many it takes to go around your cowl one time). Weave in and out of every fifth hole. Either sew together the two ends of the chain after you have woven it through the holes, or tie a knot to connect the ends.

Note: My finished cowl was approximately 16 inches in length and 9 inches wide. If you want a smaller cowl, go down in needle size or cast on 80 or 90 stitches instead of 100.

There are "friends" who destroy each other, but a real friend
sticks closer than a brother.

Proverbs 18:24 NLT

Dear Lord, Thank You for my spiritual brothers and sisters in Christ. I ask that whoever receives this gift will continue to grow in their faith and be a blessing to those around them. I praise You that You brought us together for our faith walk that has and is leading us closer to You. It is in the name of Jesus that I pray these things. Amen.

POCKET SCARF

This pattern has been a favorite gift I have given over the years to elementary school-age girls, but you could easily make it with different colors to fit a boy as well. I wish I would have had the foresight to use this as a ministry tool. There are so many young children who are bullied or feel left out while at recess, during lunch, or walking to school. This pocket scarf serves as a reminder that somebody cares for them.

Do you volunteer, teach at a school, or have a young child/grandchild/niece/nephew this age? If so, you know someone you could bless with this gift. Or the child could share this gift with another child as a sign of compassion for those who aren't always included.

Sewing a cross charm inside of the pocket adds a tangible reminder that God is with them. They can touch the cross and pray when they are being excluded or not treated with kindness. A broken and hurting child will receive comfort when they feel the cross, as well as be reminded of God's love for them.

SKILL LEVEL ♡

MATERIALS

Size US 15 (10 mm) straight needles

1 skein super bulky yarn, red*

1 skein super bulky yarn, your choice for main color*

Cross charm

Needle and thread

Stitch marker

You will need approximately 87 yards for your main color. I used Lion Brand Wool-Ease Thick & Quick yarn for both colors.

CARE INSTRUCTIONS

Machine wash in cold water, delicate cycle; air dry.

DIRECTIONS

This is a super easy and quick project done in garter stitch. With red yarn, CO 11 stitches. Knit for 5 inches. (For me, that was 21 rows.)

At 5 inches, switch to MC. Place a stitch marker on this side of the piece, to show it is the RS of the piece.

The MC yarn I used had 87 yards in the skein, so when I got to the end of that skein, on the RS of the piece, I switched to my red yarn. (The length of my MC was 40 inches.) With red yarn, knit for 5 inches. BO.

On the WS of the piece fold up both red ends. Using the red yarn, sew up the sides of both pockets and turn right side out. At Hobby Lobby, I found a charm with a cross on it that I sewed inside one of the pockets. I also laminated the Scripture and put it in the pocket as well.

I am always with you; you hold me by my right hand.

Psalm 73:23

Dear Lord, open the eyes of the children who will receive this gift so they can see their value in Your eyes and not in the eyes of their peers. I ask that when they feel as if they are an outcast, You will empower them to lift up this feeling to You. When they put their hands in their pockets, let them feel the warmth of Your love that is holding them by their right hand. I pray these things in the mighty name of Jesus. Amen.

DOUBLE SEED STITCH
NECK WARMER

The church I attend emphasizes the importance of having "relationships that matter" (RTM) and stresses how critical it is to have these level-10 (RTM) friendships. These are friends whom you can tell anything. They don't judge, yet they hold you accountable, especially if they know you are headed in the wrong direction. You know they will be praying for you and your struggles.

These friendships are resilient despite the miles that can sometimes separate you. They keep you from becoming isolated. Do you have special friends like this who need to know how much they mean to you? This neck warmer would be the ideal gift for those friends.

With online shopping, getting a package on your front porch is no big deal. However, when you see a package on your porch with a hand-written label, you get excited because you wonder who personally sent you something. Whether it was sent locally or came from miles away, you can brighten someone's day by either mailing a package or placing one on a front porch to let them know how special they are.

SKILL LEVEL ♡ ♡

MATERIALS

Size US 15 (10mm) straight needles

1 skein of bulky/super bulky yarn, your choice for the main color*

Red bulky/super bulky yarn for the red trim*

Size N/P crochet hook

2 buttons (Mine were 1-inch size.)

Needle and thread

*I used Lion Brand Wool-Ease Thick & Quick yarn (which had 87 yards) for both colors.

CARE INSTRUCTIONS

Machine wash in cold water, delicate cycle; air dry or tumble dry on low heat.

DIRECTIONS

Note: With seed stitch you K the P stitches, and P the K stitches (K1P1), and then alternate (P1K1) on every other row. In double seed stitch, the knits and purls are worked in pairs (K2P2) both across the row and vertically up and down the rows.

In this pattern you will do two rows of each to get the desired effect. That means rows 1 and 2 will be the same, but when you get to row 3 you will begin with P2, so you will be purling on the K stitch. Row 4 you will repeat P2K2 so when you go back to row 1 of the pattern you will be back to K2P2.

Using MC yarn, CO 20 stitches.

Rows 1 and 2: *K2P2* to end of row.

Rows 3 and 4: *P2K2* to end of row.

Repeat these 4 rows until your piece measures about 18 inches. (The width of mine was around 8½ inches.)

BO in the K2P2 pattern. Weave in ends.

Using the red yarn, SC around the entire piece. ◼️ Sew each button about 1 inch from each edge of one short side. Because this is a looser weave, you don't need button holes, which makes this piece more versatile. This allows you to choose whether you want to wear your neck warmer tight or loose. Attach a gift tag.

Confess your sins to each other and pray for each other so that you may be healed. The prayer of a righteous person is powerful and effective.

James 5:16

Dear Lord, I thank You that I have someone in my life who I am able to laugh with, pray with, and who holds me accountable to live a godly life. I pray that this gift brightens my friend's day and that when this neck warmer is worn, this friend is not only reminded of Your love, but how also how much I treasure our friendship. It is in the name of Jesus that I pray these things. Amen.

Pom-Pom
Twisted Rib Scarf

D o you know someone who is taking care of an elderly parent? Do you see her becoming tired and worn down from the constant care she is providing? Some elderly parents may not be able to show their appreciation for the love and care that their family member is providing. They may be incapable of expressing their love to others because of their illness. Some have dementia and become mean and angry toward their caregivers, while others may just be in so much pain that they unknowingly take it out on those they love.

My sister-in-law lovingly cared for her mother (my mother-in-law) during her battle with lung cancer. I watched her painstakingly care for her mom and put aside her own needs to make sure her mother was well taken care of in every way possible. I know it was not easy for my sister-in-law, and I can only hope and pray I will be able to do the same if my mother ever needs the same kind of attention.

This gift may be just the blessing that your caregiver friend or relative needs to be encouraged that God is with her and hears her prayers. This scarf is something you can easily make to show her that you notice what she is doing—and that you are there for her and appreciate all she has done.

SKILL LEVEL ♡♡

MATERIALS

Size US 15 (10 mm) straight needles

Approximately 200 yards super bulky yarn*

Leftover red yarn to make pom-poms

Small pom-pom maker (I used the Clover brand small yellow one.)

Elastic thread and needle (optional)

*I used Yarn Bee Hue IQ, which has 57 yards in each skein. It took 3½ skeins.

CARE INSTRUCTIONS

Hand-wash or machine wash in cold water, delicate cycle; air dry or tumble dry on low heat.

DIRECTIONS

This pattern is K in a 2 x 2 twisted rib. The twisted rib is made by knitting and purling in the back of each stitch on every row. ◼️

Note: The first and last stitch in each row are K normal, not in the back of the stitch as you do for the K2P2 repeat.

With MC yarn, CO 18 stitches. (If you would like a wider scarf, CO 22 or 26. I wanted a longer, skinny scarf. Mine was only 4 inches wide.)

For every row you will do the following pattern:

K1, *K2P2 through the back loop*; repeat between * and * until the last stitch, K1.

Continue this pattern until the desired length. (My scarf was 70 inches long.) When you are finished, BO all stitches and weave in ends. With red yarn, make 6 small pom-poms. When finishing each pom-pom, cut a long enough piece of yarn so that you can attach them to the ends of your scarf. Place 3 on each end. Attach a gift tag.

Note: So that my pom-poms would lie flat and even, I took a piece of elastic thread and sewed them together.

Come to me, all you who are weary and burdened, and I will give you rest. Take my yoke upon you and learn from me, for I am gentle and humble in heart, and you will find rest for your souls. For my yoke is easy and my burden is light.

Matthew 11:28-30

Dear Lord, I ask that You give the caregiver the words and guidance to help navigate her aging parent's needs. Give her the wisdom to not take on more burden than she can carry. Lead her to others who can help share her load. I pray that You remove any feelings of guilt when someone else is able to assist with the caretaking needs. When she feels weary and burdened, let her be reminded that You can give her the needed rest for her soul. It is in the name of Jesus that I pray these things. Amen.

For the Home

COFFEE CUP COZY

How many people do you cross paths with on a daily basis who could use some encouragement? Do you see people in the workforce serving each other? Is the only acknowledgment they receive the top of a head staring down at a phone? Sadly, for some, the only eye contact or recognition they are given occurs hours after an exhausting day on their feet.

This garter stitch coffee cup cozy can be whipped up in 30 minutes or less. I buy inexpensive reusable coffee cups or tumblers at my local dollar store, and I include a gift card inside. I have given gift cards from a local coffee shop, favorite restaurant, or nearby movie theater.

Not only is this a quick gift to knit, it's also one that you can keep in your purse to have ready in the event that God lays someone on your heart to bless. Someone who has served you in some way deserves a bit of extra recognition for the job they are doing, and this coffee cup cozy is a warm way to say thank-you.

SKILL LEVEL ♡ ♡

MATERIALS

Size US 8 (5 mm) straight needles

Worsted weight yarn, red*

Worsted weight yarn, your choice for main color*

Yarn needle

Size H crochet hook

Since this project doesn't require a lot of yarn, I used leftover worsted weight scrap yarn that I had.

CARE INSTRUCTIONS

Hand-wash in cold water; air dry.

DIRECTIONS

With MC yarn, CO 36 stitches, leaving a tail long enough to sew the ends together.

K every row until your piece measures 1½ inches.

Next row: K6, K2tog 4 times, ending with K4 (32 stitches)

Knit 2 to 3 more rows until your piece measures 2 inches.

Next row: K5, K2tog 4 times, ending with K4. (28 stitches)

Knit even for 1 more inch until your piece measures 3 inches from top to bottom. BO.

Using the red yarn and crochet hook, SC around both the top and bottom edges of your piece. ■◁ Using the tail from your CO, sew both ends together. Weave in ends.

Attach your gift tag. (I like to tie my tag to the hole on the coffee cup lid that I include with my knitted gift.)

Instead, let the Spirit renew your thoughts and attitudes.

Ephesians 4:23 NLT

Dear Lord, open my eyes to those who are serving me on a daily basis, especially those who don't see their job as making a difference. I pray that this gift renews their spirit and purpose in life. Lord, everyone needs to feel as if they matter. Let this gift be a reminder to the recipient that they make a difference. It is in the name of Jesus that I pray these things. Amen.

CHUNKY
THROW BLANKET

Though I was raised in the church, when my first husband died, I really didn't know the Lord. The day before his funeral, a neighbor's daughter wrote a poem for me about John being with God. It was the most beautiful poem and gave me so much comfort to read when I was having a hard day. She had no idea whether I was a Christian or not, yet in faith and boldness, she wrote and gave me the poem. All these years later, her written words are still meaningful to me. I don't think people realize how much hope their words can give to broken and hurting people.

Can you think of someone who sent you a text or email or gave you a handwritten note that gave you hope when you were feeling hopeless? Maybe they also included a Scripture verse that came to mind, and it was exactly the one you needed to cling to for that day. This throw blanket would be a reminder of not only the solace that you offer them, but also the comfort they have available to them from their heavenly Father.

SKILL LEVEL ♡

MATERIALS

Size US 50 (25 mm) 40-inch circular needle

Super bulky yarn, red (28 yards)*

Super bulky yarn, your choice for main color (224 yards)*

I used Hobby Lobby's Yarn Bee Eternal Bliss for both colors and needed 8 skeins for the main color.

CARE INSTRUCTIONS

Machine wash in cool water on delicate cycle; tumble dry on low.

DIRECTIONS

With red yarn, CO 34 stitches.

Row 1: K.

Row 2: switch to MC, K. Mark as RS.

With MC, continue knitting in garter stitch until you are near the end of the skein, ending with a RS row (for me this was on my eighth skein).

Switch to red yarn. Knit 2 rows in red, BO, and weave in ends.

The blanket shown in the photo is 50 inches x 50 inches. To make this blanket 45 inches x 45 inches, you would CO 30 stitches. Attach a gift tag.

Comfort, comfort my people, says your God.

Isaiah 40:1

Dear Lord, I thank You for people You have put in my life who have written words that have spoken hope into my hurting heart. When the Holy Spirit prompts me to reach out to someone, I ask that You give me the boldness to step out in faith and share Your words and Your heart with them. It is in the name of Jesus that I pray these things. Amen.

LAP BLANKET

*T*have a hard time parting with my little balls of leftover yarn. It seems that I never have quite enough left to make a small project, but I don't want to throw the yarn away. This lap blanket is the perfect project to not only deplete my yarn stash, but also to bless a nursing home with this gift for one of their residents. This is the perfect size for those in a wheelchair or for those in a recliner watching TV. Older people generally tend to be cold, so a gift like this is always welcome.

I think part of the reason I have a heart for the geriatric population is from my involvement with Widowed Persons Services. At the age of 28, as a widowed, pregnant single mom, I walked through the doors of one of their support group meetings. Everyone at that meeting loved me and embraced me. While they may have been 30 to 50 years older than I was, they still knew the pain of the death of a spouse. I won't ever forget their kindness, and I see a project like this as one way for me to give back to those who may not always have people giving to them.

This is a great project to use up some of the yarn that has been piling up in a closet. I used all different weights of yarn for this blanket. Where I had some thinner yarns, as I knit, I would use double strands of yarn to make it thicker. If you have any eyelash yarn to double with another yarn, the ladies really like the look and feel of it.

SKILL LEVEL ♡♡

MATERIALS

Leftover yarn in various coordinating colors

Red yarn (You will need enough to knit the first and last 3 rows.)

Size US 11 (8mm) 36- or 40-inch circular needle

Stitch marker

Size L crochet hook (optional, if you want to crochet a border)

DIRECTIONS

A lap blanket is anywhere from 35 x 40 inches to 36 x 45 inches (this is standard for nursing homes) or anywhere in between, so make it whatever width/length you would like. The one I made was approximately 35 x 40 inches.

CO 100 to 110 stitches in red. K 3 rows.

Beginning with Row 4, you will begin using your leftover yarn. This will be the RS of the piece, and I like to place a stitch marker to help me remember. Continue in garter stitch (knitting every row) until your piece measures 34 to 35 inches wide, ending with a WS row.

Switch to the red yarn you used on the first 3 rows. K4 rows in red, BO. Weave in all of your ends.

CARE INSTRUCTIONS

As long as you aren't using any wool yarn scraps in this blanket, you should be able to machine wash in cold water on the delicate setting and tumble dry on low.

If you have used different weight yarns, your sides are going to be all wonky, but single crocheting around the edges will make the blanket more even. ◼◀

Optional: For the blanket in the photo, I used the same red that was used on the first and last three rows and single crocheted down each side. Attach a gift tag.

Israel loved Joseph more than all his children, because he was the son of his old age. Also he made him a tunic of many colors.

Genesis 37:3 NKJV

Dear Lord, please bring to mind an older person who has made an impact on my life. Or lead me to a nursing home where I can donate this blanket to someone who needs a tangible reminder that You hear their prayers and that they are not forgotten. I ask that whoever receives this blanket will know that they are special and that You love them. It is in the name of Jesus that I pray these things. Amen.

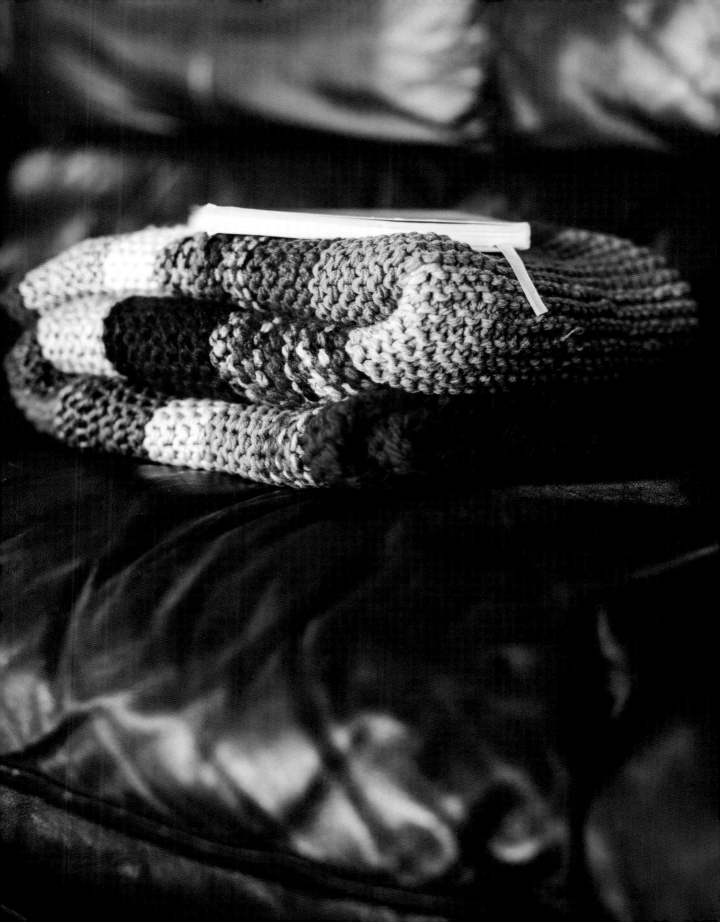

Planter Cozy

When I made this planter cozy, I envisioned giving the gift to someone who had recently moved or perhaps to a new person in the neighborhood. It can also be given to someone who has recently re-decorated their home, and you can choose your colors for this to coordinate with their new colors. Also, if you know the person doesn't have a green thumb, wrap this cozy around some kind of succulent that doesn't need much care.

When I was making this, I knew that I was going to give it to some new neighbors that had out-of-state license plates on their car. They don't live directly in my neighborhood, but I drive by their house every day. I thought this would be a good way to welcome them to not only the neighborhood, but to Texas as well. Along with the gift, I typed up the names of a local landscaper, hairstylist, barber, and some favorite local restaurants, along with my name and email address. When moving to a new area, it's always welcome to receive recommendations for needed services and, more importantly, to connect with others and start forging new friendships.

SKILL LEVEL ♡ ♡

MATERIALS

4 size US 15 (10 mm) double-pointed needles

Bulky yarn or double strands of thinner yarn, red*

Bulky yarn or double strands of thinner yarn, your choice for main color*

Stitch marker

Planter

I used double strands of Schachenmayr Boston yarn for both colors.

CARE INSTRUCTIONS

Machine wash in cold water, delicate cycle; lay flat to dry.

DIRECTIONS

With red yarn CO 32 stitches (24 for the smaller version). Divide the stitches evenly between 3 needles.

Rnd 1: Switch to MC. K1 and PM on stitch; K to end of rnd.

Rnd 2: *K1P1*; repeat to end of rnd.

You will repeat rnd 2 until your piece measures 6 inches (or less if you have a shorter pot to cover).

Switch to red yarn and K one rnd. BO and then weave in ends. Your cozy is now ready to put on your planter. I put mine on a pot containing succulents and tied my tag around one of the leaves.

Note: The larger version of this pattern fit a planter that was 6 inches in height and approximately a 19-inch circumference. The smaller version fit a pot that was 3 inches tall and 12 inches in circumference.

When you enter a house, first say, "Peace to this house."

Luke 10:5

Dear Lord, I pray for peace for the individual who will receive this gift. If they have recently moved, they may be feeling overwhelmed with unpacking and getting acclimated to their new surroundings. I pray that if they are searching for a church family, please lead them to one where they can grow. I pray for their home to be a peaceful haven. It is in the name of Jesus that I pray these things. Amen.

Beverage Cozies

While drinking kombucha may just be another fad, it's something I genuinely enjoy. I'm no Arnold Schwarzenegger, but there have been many times when I set my glass bottle on the counter a little too hard and thought, Oh, *that could have broken.* And then, *I need to knit some kind of felted cozy for this.*

Not only does this cozy keep my kombucha from breaking, now I can also bring it in the car so that the bottle doesn't get hot or sweat. Although my initial pattern was for kombucha, it can easily hold a water bottle or other beverage in a glass container as well. This pattern can also stretch to fit a pint glass.

This got me thinking…like kombucha, craft beers are also quite the rage. Are there any workers at a craft brewery whom you could bless with this? Jesus ministered to people everywhere He went. As His followers, we are called to do the same. The pattern below has modifications to make a can and smaller bottle cozy as well.

SKILL LEVEL ♡ ♡ ♡

MATERIALS

4 size 8 (5 mm) double-pointed needles

100% wool worsted weight yarn, red

100% wool worsted weight yarn, your choice for the main color

Row counter

Stitch marker

CARE INSTRUCTIONS

Hand-wash in cold water; air dry.

DIRECTIONS

With red yarn, CO 6 stitches and divide evenly among 3 needles. This is tricky because it's hard to knit with only 2 stitches on each needle, but once you get enough stitches on each of the 3 needles, it isn't awkward.

Rnd 1: K1, PM on first needle only, K to end of rnd.

Rnd 2: KFB every stitch. (12 stitches)

Rnd 3: K.

Rnd 4: *KFB, K1*; repeat until end. (18 stitches)

Rnd 5: K.

Rnd 6: *KFB, K2*; repeat until end. (24 stitches)

Rnd 7: K.

Rnd 8: *KFB, K2*; repeat until end. (32 stitches)

Rnd 9: K.

Rnd 10: *KFB, K3*; repeat until end. (40 stitches)

Rnds 11-14: K.

Rnd 15: Switch to MC yarn, K.

Continue knitting every stitch for approximately 5 inches (for kombucha-size bottle), 4½ inches (for bottle), and 3½ inches (for a can).

Switch to the red yarn and K4 rows. BO; weave in ends. Now you are ready to felt! Felting instructions are on page 11.

When you are done felting, make sure you put the wet piece on whatever bottle, glass, or can it will be used on so that it will form to that shape. Because felt acts as an insulator, these are great at keeping your beverage cool and preventing that extra condensation.

When your gift is dry, you will need to use a safety pin to attach your gift tag to it.

Whoever drinks the water I give them will never thirst. Indeed, the water I give them will become in them a spring of water welling up to eternal life.

John 4:14

Dear Lord, I thank You that You are my Living Water, and I shall not go thirsty because of this precious gift. Whether I give away this cozy for someone to hold their water bottle, kombucha, or a pint of beer, I ask that they be receptive to accepting this gift. I pray that if they don't know You, Lord, that when they use this cozy that they are reminded of who gave it to them and that they matter in Your kingdom. It is in the name of Jesus that I pray these things. Amen.

Pom-Pom Flower Bouquet in Yarn-Wrapped Vase

*I*n this book, I have tried to include a few gift ideas that don't require actual knitting skills. This is definitely one of them. Let me emphasize: This is REALLY easy to do. In fact, once you make one of these, you are going to be inspired to keep on gifting these bouquets to people you know—and even those you don't!

My initial idea behind making and giving this gift away was to bless a receptionist. This particular job doesn't receive a lot of recognition. I see people staring down at their phones as they check in at appointments without even acknowledging the hard worker behind the desk.

Unfortunately, many people also take out their frustrations on receptionists as well. This especially happens when the doctor or dentist or whomever they have their appointment with is running late. What would happen if you showed a receptionist or someone else who works with the public some extra kindness and let them know you appreciate them and that they matter in God's kingdom? Wouldn't this fun gift put a smile on their faces to let them know that you noticed them today?

SKILL LEVEL ♡

MATERIALS

Pom-pom maker

Package of 3/16-inch x 12-inch wooden dowels

Small vase

Scrap yarn in red

Scrap yarn in your color or colors of choice for main color to wrap around vase

Spray adhesive

E6000 permanent craft adhesive

Old English Scratch Cover (optional)

Modeling clay (optional)

CARE INSTRUCTIONS

No need to water these flowers!

DIRECTIONS

Using spray adhesive, spray 1-inch portions of the vase to wrap your yarn. The spray goes everywhere, so I recommend doing it outside or covering a table with newspaper or a disposable cloth. With red yarn, starting at the bottom, wrap 1 inch. Switch colors and continue wrapping the rest of the vase, or alternate colors to make stripes. (I used a variegated yarn for my vase, which gave the appearance of color changes.) When you are almost done, switch back to the red yarn for the last 4 or 5 wraps.

The size of vase you use will determine how many pom-pom flowers you will need to make. Again, this is a great way to use up leftover yarn. Because of my color scheme, I stained my wooden dowels using some Old English Scratch Cover. I also wanted my flower "stems" different heights, so that is where the modeling clay came in for me. You could cut the stems in varying lengths, but for me it was easier to adjust the height of the stems by adding modeling clay at the bottom of the dowels.

When you are finished making the pom-poms 📹, use the E6000 glue (make sure you read the directions on this glue because it has to set) to attach them to the top of the wooden dowels. Attach a gift tag to one of the flower stems.

May the favor of the Lord our God rest on us; establish the work of our hands for us— yes, establish the work of our hands.

Psalm 90:17

Dear Lord, I ask that You show favor on the staff that will receive this gift. Bless them by putting people in their paths who appreciate their hard work. Open their eyes to see that You have established the work of their hands to bless others. It is in the name of Jesus that I pray these things. Amen.

LAVENDER SACHET

If you've never had severe anxiety, it is hard to empathize with someone who suffers from it. Their anxious thoughts don't make sense to you. However irrational those thoughts may seem, though, these thoughts are their reality. Sometimes all it takes to help someone with anxiety is to show empathy, listen to them, and redirect their negative thinking to more positive thoughts. And this gift of a lavender sachet can help.

Recently, my mother has been dealing with anxiety, which causes her blood pressure to rise. I felt God nudge me to share prayers and verses with her that have helped me calm my own anxious thoughts. These prayers and Scriptures have guided me to redirect my focus from myself to my Lord and Savior.

The scent of lavender is calming to me. My mother loves the color purple, so this pattern was inspired by her. I envision her putting this sachet next to her morning devotionals to enjoy during her quiet time. You can include a bottle of lavender essential oil with this gift to refresh the sachet. In addition to Proverbs 12:25, you could also list some of your other favorite Scriptures that comfort you when you're feeling anxious or stressed.

SKILL LEVEL ♡ ♡

MATERIALS

4 size US 10 (6 mm) double-pointed needles

Worsted weight yarn, red and your choice for the main color*

Row counter

Size G crochet hook

2-3 tablespoons of dried lavender

Small organza drawstring bag (optional)

This project doesn't require a great deal of yarn, so I used left-over cotton yarn.

CARE INSTRUCTIONS

Machine wash in cold water; air dry or tumble dry, low heat.

DIRECTIONS

With red yarn, CO 24 stitches and divide the stitches evenly between 3 of the needles.

Rnds 1-2: K.

Rnds 3-25: Switch to MC; K.

Rnds 26-28: Switch to red yarn; K.

You will BO using the 3-needle BO. To set up for this, move the stitches so that you have 12 stitches on each of 2 needles, using your third needle for your BO. Turn your piece inside out, then begin your 3-needle BO. ◼️ You will need a 12-inch tie to close the bag. You can either make a crochet chain, an I-cord, or use a piece of ribbon to make your tie. I crocheted the chain with the MC yarn for mine. For the lavender, you can either place it directly in the pouch or fill a small organza drawstring pouch to put inside of the bag. Fasten your tie around the top of the bag. Attach a gift tag.

Anxiety weighs down the heart, but a kind word cheers it up.

Proverbs 12:25

Dear Lord, I ask that the person receiving this sachet not only experiences the calmness from the smell, but also soaks in Your peace as they are reminded that anxiety will weigh down their thoughts. Lift them out of negative thinking and turn their anxious thoughts to You. I pray that they listen to Your peaceful voice and not to the voice of the enemy. It is in the name of Jesus that I pray these things. Amen.

FELTED COASTERS

Some people seem to have a knack for entertaining. Sometimes you may even feel guilty because it feels as if you are always going to their house. Don't feel guilty; bring them a hand-knit gift instead! Some people just have the gift of hospitality. If that gift isn't yours, that's fine because God has given you your own unique gifts to serve others.

These coasters are a quick knit. In fact, you can easily make several to take along to your next gathering. When your friends and family welcome guests into their home, I am sure they appreciate people using coasters so that their tables don't become ruined from wet glasses that are set on them. This gift is a nice gesture to show how much you appreciate them opening their home to others on a regular basis.

SKILL LEVEL ♡ ♡ ♡

MATERIALS

4 size US 11 (8 mm) 7-inch double-pointed needles

100% wool worsted weight yarn, red and your choice for main color

Row counter

Stitch marker

Yarn needle

CARE INSTRUCTIONS

Hand-wash in cold water; lay flat to dry.

DIRECTIONS

Using MC, CO 8 stitches. Divide stitches evenly on 3 needles (I did 3, 2, 3). The first rnd is a bit awkward, but once you knit the first rnd, it gets easier. Your increase rows (where the KFBs are worked) are the odd rows.

Rnd 1: KFB in every stitch. (16 stitches)

Rnd 2: K. (I placed a stitch marker on the yarn on the first needle to remind me to click on my row counter when I finished a rnd.)

Rnd 3: *KFB, K1*; repeat to end of rnd. (24 stitches)

Rnd 4: K.

Rnd 5: *KFB K2*; repeat to end of rnd. (32 stitches)

Rnd 6: K.

Rnd 7: *KFB, K3*; repeat to end of rnd. (40 stitches)

Rnd 8: K.

Rnd 9: *KFB, K4* repeat to end of rnd. (48 stitches)

Rnd 10: Switch to red yarn. K.

Rnd 11: *KFB, K5*; repeat to end of rnd. (56 stitches)

Rnd 12: Add a second strand of red yarn and BO purlwise.

Note: Do not skip the double strand of yarn for the BO, because this is what creates the cupped edging.

You will need to sew the BO and CO area closed. Using the center yarn, cinch and sew the hole closed. Sew up any other holes you might have, because they will show after felting. It is now ready to felt. Instructions for felting are on page 11.

This is a good way to use up any scrap wool yarn you may have. If you are using a new skein of yarn, you can get several coasters made out of it. I put each coaster in its own zippered bag for felting. Once it is the size you would like, you will need to stretch the coaster a bit all the way around to get the round shape. They are not going to look like perfect circles when you take them out of the bags, so I set a wine glass on top of each coaster and pulled the fabric around the stem end of the glass to make the circle shape and then allowed the coasters to dry. Attach a gift tag.

If you know how to needle felt, ◼◀ these coasters can quickly and easily have a design such as a monogram, special word or phrase, or simple decoration dry felted on them to make them more personal.

Each of you should use whatever gift you have received to serve others, as faithful stewards of God's grace in its various forms.

1 Peter 4:10

Dear Lord, I thank You for those who have a heart for welcoming friends, families, and neighbors into their home. I ask that You continue to bless them with opportunities to minister to others in this way. If they feel discouraged that no one else volunteers their home for fellowship or entertaining, help them to see that You will provide rest, food, and time for preparation. It is in the name of Jesus that I pray these things. Amen.

CELL PHONE BASKET

When you're good friends with your next-door neighbors, that's always a blessing. It's a double blessing when your son and their daughter fall in love and get married. My next-door neighbors, who are also my son's in-laws, often host family get-togethers.

However, my husband and I usually host Thanksgiving dinner for my family at our house. But a few years ago, my daughter had been diagnosed with thyroid cancer, and my mother-in-law was dying from lung cancer. Having a Thanksgiving dinner at our house was not something we were wanting to do. Our neighbors welcomed us all over with open arms.

One day while on a walk with my son's mother-in-law, we were venting about how frustrating it is to have a family gathering and watch everyone stare at their phones. She declared that at the next holiday event, she was going to have a cell phone basket, and everyone had to drop their phone in it as they walked through the door. Our conversation is what inspired this pattern.

This cell phone basket is perfect for anyone who routinely hosts events at their house. While my neighbor came to mind as I made this, it doesn't have to be for a family member or friend to use at home. A Bible study, small group, or youth group leader could be blessed with this basket to use at their next meeting or event.

This basket is also multifunctional and can be used for more than cell phones. It could easily hold keys or sunglasses. It's up to your imagination!

SKILL LEVEL ♡♡♡

MATERIALS

Size US 15 (10 mm) 24-inch circular needle

4 size US 15 (10mm) double-pointed needles

Heat-fusible craft cord in red and your choice for the main color*

Lighter (to fuse the cord)

Knitting needle point protectors

*I used Bonnie Craft Cord for both colors of the craft cord.

DIRECTIONS

Using the thumb cast-on method, CO 50 stitches with red craft cord. Make sure the end of your cast-on piece is fused so it doesn't unravel. You will be working this project from the top down.

Rnd 1: K.

Rnd 2: P.

After Rnd 2, switch to MC. You will need to fuse the end of the red cording to the end of the MC cording before starting Rnd 3.

Rnd 3: K6, BO6, K19, BO6, K13.

Rnd 4: K6, CO6, K19, CO6, K13. (Use thumb CO for the CO stitches.)

Make sure you pull the cording tight between the first and last CO stitches of the handles.

Rnds 5-10: K.

For the base, you can continue in the MC, or for contrast, switch back to the red. If you choose to have the red on the bottom as I did, cut the MC cording and fuse it to the red cording before you start your decrease rows. I'm not going to lie—while I love the look of the basket made with this craft cord, the first time I knit with it, I struggled with the decrease portion. This is where I used my needle point protectors to keep the cording on the ends of my double-pointed needles so that the stitches wouldn't fall off of the needles as I was decreasing stitches.

Decrease rnds. (Switch to your double points when it is too hard to knit on the circulars. For me it was after rnd 6.)

Rnd 1: *K3, K2tog*; repeat to end of rnd. (40 stitches)

Rnds 2-3: K.

Rnd 4: *K2, K2tog*; repeat to end of rnd. (30 stitches)

Rnd 5: K.

Rnd 6: *K1 K2tog*; repeat to end of rnd. (20 stitches)

Rnd 7: K.

Rnd 8: *K2 tog*; repeat to end of rnd. (10 stitches)

Rnd 9: K.

Cut a 12-inch tail and pull through those last 10 stitches. Pull the cording to the inside of the piece; cut the cord and fuse it so it won't unravel. Attach a gift tag.

Share with the Lord's people who are in need. Practice hospitality.

Romans 12:13

Dear Lord, I thank You for giving the recipient of this cell phone basket the gift of hospitality. Continue to be with them as they reach out to those in need of welcoming arms. Bless their hands as they prepare for the gatherings that they host and help them to create a spirit of community. It is in the name of Jesus that I pray these things. Amen.

BLESSING BOWL

*D*o you know someone who is feeling as if the weight of the world is on their shoulders? Are they feeling overwhelmed with all they have to do to make ends meet and accomplish each day's tasks? Maybe it's a single mom or a college student who comes to mind. Or a friend who is unemployed or unsure of their future. This blessing bowl can help this individual take their eyes off their circumstances and turn them instead to their heavenly Father.

What makes this a blessing bowl is the rocks you will provide for the person you're giving it to. Ask them to write on these rocks how God has been faithful to them in the past. When they are feeling discouraged, these rocks will serve as reminders of how God has, is, and will continue to provide for them.

This would have been the perfect gift for someone to have given me when I was a young, widowed single mom. There were many days when something like this would have been a tangible reminder of God's love for me.

If you live somewhere where you can handpick rocks for this basket, you will save money. Otherwise, you can purchase a bag of rocks from a local craft store or order some online to include with this gift.

SKILL LEVEL ♡ ♡ ♡

MATERIALS

Size US 13 (9 mm) 16-inch circular needle

4 size US 13 (9 mm) double-pointed needles

1 skein 100% wool worsted weight yarn, red*

1 skein 100% wool worsted weight yarn, your choice of color*

Stitch marker

Row counter

Yarn needle

River rocks

Sharpie marker

I used Patons Classic Wool for both colors of yarn.

DIRECTIONS

Using double strands of red yarn, CO 75 stitches. I pulled the yarn from the center and outside so that I only needed to use one skein of yarn. PM before you begin to join in the rnd, being careful to not twist your stitches.

Rnds 1-2: P.

Rnd 3: Switch to double strands of MC yarn. You will K using MC for 6 inches from CO edge.

Decrease rnds

Rnd 1: *SSK, K11, K2tog*; repeat to end of rnd. (65 stitches)

Rnd 2: K.

Rnd 3: *SSK, K9, K2tog*; repeat to end of rnd. (55 stitches)

Rnd 4: K.

Rnd 5: *SSK, K7, K2tog*; repeat to end of rnd. (45 stitches)

Rnd 6: K.

Rnd 7: *SSK, K5, K2tog*; repeat to end of rnd. (35 stitches)

Rnd 8: K. (Switch to double points to continue.)

Hand-wash in cold water; air dry.

Rnd 9: *SSK, K3, K2tog*; repeat to end of rnd. (25 stitches)

Rnd 10: K.

Rnd 11: *SSK, K1, K2tog*; repeat to end of rnd. (15 stitches)

Cut a 12-inch tail and thread your yarn needle. Pull the tail through the 15 remaining stitches. Sew down the center portion so that there aren't any small holes. Sew closed any holes or gaps because the felting process won't close them completely. I had some looser areas where I decreased that I needed to sew up. Trim and weave in any loose ends. When you are finished, it pretty much looks like a really big hat. It is now ready to felt.

Instructions for felting can be found on page 11. How long you felt it will determine how big it ends up. I wanted mine on the smaller side, so I felted it longer. My finished bowl was about 4 inches tall and 6 inches across the top portion. It took 2 washes for mine to get to the size I wanted. For drying, I found a plastic storage container at the dollar store that was the size I wanted for the felted bowl. Once it was that size, I was able to pull it around the plastic bowl so it dried in the shape I wanted. If you don't want to do this, you can stuff it with plastic grocery sacks so it will hold its shape.

Fill the dried bowl with river rocks and a silver or gold sharpie. Write Hebrews 13:8 on one of the rocks. Put your gift tag inside of the bowl.

Jesus Christ is the same yesterday and today and forever.

Hebrews 13:8

Dear Lord, thank You that You are unchanging and always faithful. Please open this person's eyes to see that You do not want or expect them to carry the weight of the world on their shoulders. Empower them with Your strength to take life one day at a time. Help the rocks in this blessing bowl to be a reminder of that. It is in the name of Jesus that I pray these things. Amen.

Kitchen, Bath, Cleaning

DISH SCRUBBY WITH MATCHING DISHCLOTH

Can you think of someone who has the not-so-glamorous job of cleaning up after people?

Maybe it's one of the janitors you see in the school halls. Or someone from the cleaning service that your workplace or church employs. Perhaps even the person bussing tables at the restaurant where you are eating. These people often don't receive much acknowledgment for keeping the places others enjoy clean.

I like to make a set of 4 to 5 of these scrubbies at a time to give away because they can get yucky from washing dishes—or occasionally they fall down the disposal and are destroyed.

When you give your gift, let the recipient know you notice them and the good job they are doing. I am sure there are days when they don't feel very appreciated. I especially think of the days when they have to go back and mop the just-cleaned floor that someone just spilled coffee on. This small gift will remind them that their work is valuable and important.

SKILL LEVEL ♡

MATERIALS

Size US 10 (6 mm) straight needles or circular needle for scrubby

Size US 8 (5mm) straight needles or circular needle for dishcloth

1 skein scrubby yarn, red*

1 skein, your choice for main color*

*I used Red Heart Scrubby Cotton for both colors of yarn.

CARE INSTRUCTIONS

Machine wash in warm water; tumble dry on medium heat. You can also put these in your dishwasher and wash when you run the dishwasher.

DIRECTIONS

DISH SCRUBBY

With double strands of red yarn (I used both ends and K double strands from the same skein), CO 15 stitches.

K 1 row in red. Switch to double strands of MC for row 2, and continue knitting rows in MC until your piece measures 4 inches. Switch back to double strands of the red yarn and K the last two rows. BO and weave in the ends.

MATCHING DISHCLOTH

The dishcloth is K using a single strand of yarn.

With red yarn, CO 36 stitches.

K one row in red.

Switch to MC. Knit for 7 inches.

Switch to red. Knit 2 rows. BO and weave in ends.

You can sausage roll your dishcloth around the scrubby. Using a red ribbon or piece of yarn, attach your gift tag and tie around your bundle.

If we walk in the light, as he is in the light, we have fellowship with one another, and the blood of Jesus, his Son, purifies us from all sin.

1 John 1:7

Dear Lord, I ask that You open my eyes to those around me who are an integral part of keeping order. I know I take it for granted that floors are mopped and toilets are cleaned at places that I frequent. I lift up the person who will receive this gift. I pray they be encouraged by Your Word. It is in the name of Jesus that I pray these things. Amen.

SMALL RUG/BATH MAT

*I*n Mark 2, four men brought a paralyzed man to Jesus to be healed. They dug a hole in the roof and dropped him down on his mat to get him to Jesus. Can you imagine having friends like that? They knew if they could get their friend to Jesus, He would heal him.

Do you have any friends in your life like that who would do anything for you? Can you think of a time when you needed help and someone you considered an acquaintance brought you a meal or offered to drive you to an appointment?

I will never forget the kindness I received from a friend when my father passed. My family called her our Fairy Godmother. It seemed as if every time we ran out of paper plates or napkins or just needed something, those items showed up on our doorstep without our even asking. She got the word out at my children's school, and people started blessing us with household items and meals—people we had never even met!

Who can you bless with this gift? Who has been a blessing to you at some time in your life? Maybe you know someone moving into a new home, or someone whose child is going off to college or moving out on their own who might need some household items. They would certainly appreciate this small rug/bath mat and your thinking of them.

SKILL LEVEL ♡

MATERIALS

Size US 19 (15mm) straight needles or circular needle

1 skein bulky yarn, red*

3 skeins bulky yarn, your choice for the main color*

I used Hobby Lobby's I Love This Chunky yarn for both colors. There are 109 yards of yarn in each skein.

CARE INSTRUCTIONS

Machine wash in cold water, delicate cycle; tumble dry on low.

DIRECTIONS

This rug is made using the broken rib stitch, which is done in multiples of 2 + 1. Using double strands of the red yarn, CO 45 stitches. (I prefer using a circular needle so I don't have to shove down my stitches.) K one row.

For row 2, switch to MC and begin the pattern below. Where you add MC will be considered the RS of the piece.

Row 2: K. (RS)

Row 3: K1P1 all the way across, ending with K1. (WS)

Continue in this pattern (row 2 and row 3) until your piece is the desired length. I wanted a square, so the one pictured is 24 x 24 inches, but you could make yours more of a rectangle. I knit mine for 23 inches, making sure I was ending on the RS of the piece. Switch to the red yarn and K 2 rows. BO and weave in ends. Attach a gift tag.

Note: I also cut a piece of nonskid rug pad to put underneath the rug and included that with the gift.

I tell you, get up, take your mat and go home.

Mark 2:11

Dear Lord, I ask that You bring to mind someone who has been a blessing to me and may not realize the impact their kindness has had on me. I pray for this person to know their worth in You and to recognize the difference that they are making in Your kingdom It is in the name of Jesus that I pray these things. Amen.

Felted Pan Sleeve and Trivet

*I*s there someone in your life who loves to cook? Lucky me—that person is my husband! While I don't mind cooking, it isn't a stress release for me like it is for him. He loves creating things without a recipe. Our family and neighbors are always willing to test his new recipes.

Using a hot pad pan holder works better than wrapping a towel or hot pad around a handle, or worse, grabbing the pan without one! Ouch! When you are cooking more than one item, it is easy to mindlessly grab the handle without using a hot pad. Because these are so quick and easy to make, you can knit several at a time before felting them. In addition, I like to make a felted square trivet to give as a companion to the pan sleeve. The recipient can place the hot pan on the trivet before they serve the food.

You can either give this gift to someone you know who loves to cook or to someone who is wanting to learn how to cook. You could also gift a cast-iron pan along with this pan sleeve and trivet for a special occasion such as a wedding or graduation.

SKILL LEVEL ♡

MATERIALS

12-peg round loom (flower loom)

Size US 15 (10mm) needles (straight or circular, your preference)

100% wool worsted weight yarn, red

100% wool worsted weight yarn, your choice for the main color

Yarn needle

Loom hook

DIRECTIONS

PAN SLEEVE

Using the e-wrap method, CO with double strands of red wool yarn. K for 2 rnds. Using double strands, switch to MC or use scrap yarn for stripes and K for Rnds 3-14. Switch back to red yarn for Rnds 15-16. BO using the basic BO in the rnd. ■◖

Turn the piece inside out, sew closed one of the ends. I sewed closed the BO end. Weave in and trim ends. It is now ready to felt. See instructions on page 11 for felting. Depending on how long you felt it, you can make multiple lengths for your pot handles. My piece was approximately 4½ x 2 inches before felting. Because this is felted, you will need to attach your gift tag with a safety pin.

CARE INSTRUCTIONS

Hand-wash or machine wash, delicate cycle in cold water; air dry.

TRIVET/HOT PAD

Using red yarn, CO 24 stitches.

Switch to MC for row 2 (this will be the RS of your piece).

K until your piece is almost 9 inches long. On the RS of the piece, you will switch back to the red yarn. K one row in red. BO. Weave in ends.

It is now ready to felt. Refer to the felting instructions on page 11. My piece before felting was 9 inches x 9 inches, and after felting it was 7 inches x 7 inches. Attach a gift tag.

Give us today our daily bread.

Matthew 6:11

Dear Lord, I thank You for those in my life who have the gift of cooking amazing meals. I ask that You bless them with peace as they create in the kitchen. While friends and family may not always seem appreciative of their cooking, I pray that they are reminded every day that You are the Bread of Life and You will give them everything they need for sustainment. It is in the name of Jesus that I pray these things. Amen.

Dust Mop Cloths

As a parent, it has always been important that I start my children at a young age contributing to the running of the family household. The chores don't have to be complicated, and they can become more challenging as the child grows. But it's important that this habit start at a young age. It helps the child learn responsibility, and it helps with family cohesiveness.

I know this was one of my daughter's least-favorite jobs, but when you have a dog that sheds, "swiffering" is a necessity. I would ask her to perform this task before I would do the wet mop portion. This was one of her regular chores that lasted until she went off to college. Many times, she wasn't able to go out until she had done it. I like to think that having a cute, hand-knit dust mop cloth makes this job a little more enjoyable.

These cloths are also an eco-friendly alternative to those throwaway cloths that you tuck into a "Swiffer"-type mop. You can use these dry or wet, so you don't need to buy two different kinds to use. Not to mention, with this gift, you aren't adding more to our landfills. These are great gifts for a parent, grandparent, or other caregiver to use with a little helper at chore time.

SKILL LEVEL ♡

MATERIALS

Size US 8 (5mm) straight needles or circular needle

1 skein cotton or cotton blend yarn, red or pink*

1 skein cotton or cotton blend yarn, your choice of color*

Yarn needle

*I used Hobby Lobby's Crafter's Choice yarn for both colors. There are 120 yards in each skein, which can make 3 cloths.

DIRECTIONS

This dust mop cloth fits 10-inch x 5-inch size mops. I have two versions of this. One is done in garter stitch and the other uses seed stitch. I was able to get 3 dust mop covers out of the 2 skeins of yarn I used.

With red yarn, CO 42 stitches. K for 2 inches. (For me, that was 15 rows.) Switch to MC yarn. This will become the RS of your piece. K for 4 inches before switching back to the red yarn.

If you would like to use seed stitch, CO 43 stitches with the red yarn. K for 2 inches. Switch to MC yarn and K one row.

Begin the seed stitch pattern as follows: K1P2 to end of the row. On the next row, P1K1 to the end of the row. Repeat these two rows (K on the P stitches, and P on the K stitches). Seed stitch creates the bumpy effect, which is really good for wet mopping.

For either the garter stitch or seed stitch mop cloth, when your piece measures 6 inches from the beginning, switch back to the red yarn and K for the last 2 inches. At this point, your piece will measure around 8 to 8½ inches. BO.

CARE INSTRUCTIONS

Machine wash in warm water; tumble dry on medium. I don't use fabric softener or dryer sheets. The more static the better using it to dry mop.

To finish this piece, with the RS facing up, fold in both red ends to the middle of the piece. Either cut a 12-inch piece of yarn or use the yarn tails on your piece to sew up the short sides of your piece (the red ends). You don't have to do this next part, but I like my dust cloth to fit snug, so I also sew up ½ to 1 inch of the red from the edge up toward the middle. Weave in loose ends. Turn your piece right side out. Attach a gift tag.

Start children off on the way they should go, and even when they are old they will not turn from it.

Proverbs 22:6

Dear Lord, help this parent, grandparent, or caregiver to train up their child in the way they should go so that they are grounded in Your Word. I pray for the person who receives this gift to not be discouraged if their child does not always have a helpful spirit. You can change anyone's heart—including a child's. It is in the name of Jesus that I pray these things. Amen.

FELTED DRYER BALLS

Do you have friends who are environmentally conscious and live a holistic lifestyle? If so, think about making a set of these wool dryer balls for their family. The beauty of this project is that you don't even need to know how to knit or use a loom. All you have to do is be able to wind a ball of yarn!

One way to show your support to those who wish to recycle as much as possible is to give them a set of dryer balls. They may have these already, but if you are drying a set of king-size sheets, you really need more than two to fluff out the wrinkles.

Maybe you're the environmental one and would like to see others being more conscious of taking care of our planet. You can give this gift along with some essential oils that provide a natural fresh scent to just-washed laundry. Lavender is one of my favorites because of the calming effect it has, but you may have another favorite scent to include.

SKILL LEVEL ♡

MATERIALS

100% wool yarn (not superwash, as it will not felt)

Crochet hook or tapestry/yarn needle

Old tights or pantyhose

Essential oils (optional)

CARE INSTRUCTIONS

Use over and over in your dryer. If you would like, sprinkle with your favorite essential oil.

DIRECTIONS

Using your thumb and pinky finger, wrap your yarn in a figure 8 around those 2 fingers. ▶ Once you have a good chunk on those fingers, fold in half and start wrapping your yarn around it to form a ball about the size of a tennis ball. When you are getting to the size you want, add in some red yarn to finish it off to keep our red theme. Cut the yarn, thread through your needle, and weave the tail back and forth several times in different directions to secure it to the ball so it doesn't unravel. Make several dryer balls at a time—they're quick and easy!

Cut the leg off of a pair of tights or pantyhose. Roll the first ball down to the toe, securely tie a knot, add your next yarn ball and do the same. Continue doing this until you are done tying them all. Wash the dryer balls on the hottest water setting and dry them on your highest setting. If you don't want to waste water, wash them with a load of dark towels or rags. When they are dry, cut off the pantyhose, sprinkle them with your favorite essential oils, and they are ready to give as a gift! You can tie your gift tag around the bottle of essential oil.

**The heavens are yours,
and the earth is yours;
everything in the
world is yours—you
created it all.**

Psalm 89:11 NLT

*Dear Lord, I ask that You give the recipient of this gift the ability
and the resources to stay strong in their convictions of being environmentally conscious. Give them wisdom on what they can do to
impact those around them to follow their example. Lord, if they
don't know You, continue to draw them to You. It is in the name of
Jesus that I pray these things. Amen.*

MINI FACIAL COTTON PADS WITH POUCH

*J*ust as God put Adam in the Garden of Eden to tend and care for it, we should also be doing what we can to keep our world beautiful. I know it is much easier to buy cotton pads to remove makeup, but this pattern is a good alternative, especially for someone who is passionate about saving our planet.

Do you have friends or family members who are careful to recycle and use products that don't add to our landfills? If so, these cotton pads with a matching pouch would be perfect for them. They are made in solid white so that they can be bleached if needed. The carrying pouch to store them has the red color on it to serve as a reminder of Jesus's love.

I also like to include with this gift some homemade facial toner using equal parts of apple cider vinegar and filtered water or a bottle of premade facial toner.

SKILL LEVEL ♡ ♡ ♡

MATERIALS

MINI FACIAL COTTON PADS

Size US 8 (5 mm) straight needles

Size US 8 (5 mm) 9-inch circular needle

Size US 8 double-pointed needles or size G/H crochet hook (to make the drawstring)

Cotton yarn, white*

Row counter

Cotton yarn, red*

Stitch marker

I used Hobby Lobby's I Love This Cotton because it is so soft.

DIRECTIONS

MINI FACIAL COTTON PADS

With white yarn, CO 12 stitches. K for 18 rows (or until your piece measures 2½ inches). BO and weave in ends. Mine were approximately 2½ x 2½ inches.

Make 12 facial cotton pads for the pouch.

POUCH

With red yarn and circular needle, CO 14 stitches. K for 20 rows. Pick up 14 stitches from each of the three sides for a total of 56 stitches on your needle. This will form the square bottom of your bag . 🎥

Place a marker at the beginning of the rnd and K for 3 more rnds.

Switch to the white yarn and continue knitting for 20 more rnds. (My piece measured 3½ inches from the bottom.)

Row 24: *K4, YO*; repeat to the end of the rnd, ending with a YO.

Row 25: *K2tog, K3*; repeat to the end of the rnd, ending with K3.

K for 8 more rnds. BO; weave in ends.

For the drawstring, I prefer the look of the I-cord, but you can also crochet a chain that is 16 inches in length.

CARE INSTRUCTIONS

Machine wash in warm water, normal cycle; tumble dry on low or medium heat. Can use bleach if needed on the facial pads.

For the I-cord as shown in the photo, using your double-pointed needles, CO 3 stitches with the red yarn. K for 16 inches. ▉◀

After you finish your I-cord, trim the ends, weave through the holes (you should have 8 holes), and tie a bow. Attach your gift tag.

Note: You could also use red ribbon to weave through the holes for your drawstring.

The LORD God took the man and put him in the Garden of Eden to work it and take care of it.

Genesis 2:15

Dear Lord, I thank You for people who are doing whatever they can to lessen waste on this planet. Continue to encourage this person to not feel defeated when she sees others not caring for the earth as she does. We are called to tend to our corner of the world where we live, so please continue to use this person to impress the importance of this truth on those around them. It is in the name of Jesus that I pray these things. Amen.

EXFOLIATING SOAP SOCK

The tween years can be an awkward time. I remember that when my daughter was in middle school, it was sometimes hard for her to feel as if she fit in, especially because we moved midyear, and she found herself having to make a whole new set of friends.

Not only is it difficult for a girl this age to try to discover who she is, but it is also hard for her to stand firm in her faith because of peers who will mock her for being a goody-goody if she does the right thing when everyone around her is making poor choices. Can you think of a young girl who is going through this stage of life and could use this reminder that God is with her, will strengthen and help her, and will uphold her with His right hand?

When she uses this exfoliating soap sock, not only will she be reminded of your love and prayers for her, but also that God is with her wherever she goes.

SKILL LEVEL ♡ ♡ ♡

MATERIALS

4 size US 10 (6mm) double-pointed needles

Cotton scrubby yarn*

Size G crochet hook

Bar of soap

*Hobby Lobby's Scrub-ology Cotton or Red Heart Scrubby Cotton are what I use.

CARE INSTRUCTIONS

Machine wash in cool or warm water; tumble dry on medium heat.

DIRECTIONS

Using the red yarn, CO 32 stitches. Divide evenly between 3 needles. (I divided the stitches 11, 10, 11 per needle.)

Rnd 1: K.

Rnds 2-10: Switch to MC; K.

Rnd 11: *K4, YO*; repeat, ending with a YO.

Rnd 12: *K2tog, K3*; repeat, ending with a K2.

Rnds 13-30: K.

Rnds 31-33: Switch to red yarn, K.

You will use the 3-needle BO. Put 16 stitches on each of your 2 needles, using your third needle for your BO. Make sure you turn your piece inside out to do this. ■◢

You will need a 16-inch tie to cinch the top closed. You can either crochet a chain or make an I-cord using either the red or MC yarn. ■◢ If doing an I-cord, you will CO 3 stitches. Weave your tie through the holes and tie a bow. I know that the finished product looks loose, baggy, and way too big for your bar of soap. This is why it is important for you to wash and dry the soap sock before you put your soap in it. Wash the sock in warm water and dry on medium heat. It is going to shrink up to the perfect size after you do that. Put your soap in the sock and tie a bow. Attach your gift tag.

Do not fear, for I am with you; do not be dismayed, for I am your God. I will strengthen you and help you; I will uphold you with my righteous right hand.

Isaiah 41:10

Dear Lord, I ask that this young lady be able to stay grounded in Your Word, despite those who might mock her. Let her feel Your strength to stand firm on the Foundation in which she has been raised. When she feels discouraged, allow her to feel You holding her hand and helping her get through a difficult day. It is in the name of Jesus that I pray these things. Amen.

TRINITY STITCH WASHCLOTH

The Trinity stitch symbolizes the Father, Son, and Holy Spirit. As I make these Trinity stitch washcloths, I always pray that God will show me who should receive them.

While my husband and I were on a flight to New York, the plane hit some pretty bad weather, causing quite a bit of turbulence. The woman sitting behind us was having a hard time. She was holding on to her husband and crying. The flight attendant even went by her side to try to comfort her. If I'd had one of these washcloths with me, I could have handed it to her and shared with her the story of the Trinity stitch as well as the prayer I prayed for her as I knit it. Not only could she have used this cloth to wipe her tears, but she could have also gripped it in one of her hands to release some of her tension.

This is a gift you can give to anyone who needs to wipe away their tears and be reminded of the love of the Father, Son, and Holy Spirit. It's a small item you can keep in your purse and easily give away at any time you feel led by the Spirit to do so. Because of the calming effect of lavender, I also like to spritz mine using a scented spray.

SKILL LEVEL ♡ ♡

MATERIALS

Size US 8 (5mm) straight needles

1 skein cotton yarn, red, and 1 skein of your choice for the main color*

Stitch marker

Row counter

One skein of the cotton yarn will make 3 to 4 washcloths. I used Hobby Lobby's I Love This Cotton for both colors.

CARE INSTRUCTIONS

Machine wash in warm water; tumble dry on low/medium heat.

DIRECTIONS

If you aren't sure how to do the Trinity stitch, please refer to KnitPrayShare.com. ◼️ Your increase stitch is a K1, P1, K1 in the same stitch, so you are knitting 3 stitches in that one stitch.

Using the red yarn, CO 32 stitches.

Switch to your MC for Row 1.

Rows 1-4: K all rows. (I placed my stitch marker on row 3 to remind me that it was the RS of the piece.)

Row 5: (RS) K4, P24, K4.

Row 6: K4 *K1, P1, K1 in the same stitch, P3tog*; repeat 6 times, K4.

Row 7: (RS) K4, P24, K4.

Row 8: K4 *P3tog, K1, P1, K1 in the same stitch*; repeat 6 times, K4.

Repeat Rows 5-8 for 8 repeats.

After your eighth repeat of the Trinity stitch pattern, K4 rows. On the fifth row, switch to the red yarn and K 1 row.

BO. Weave in ends. Attach your gift tag.

He is exalted to the place of highest honor in heaven, at God's right hand. And the Father, as he had promised, gave him the Holy Spirit to pour out upon us, just as you see and hear today.

Acts 2:33 NLT

Dear Lord, I ask that You bless the person who will receive this gift with a spirit of calmness. Replace any anxious feelings with peace. Help them find true serenity and comfort regardless of the fears residing in their heart. When they use this washcloth, bring an awareness of Your presence and the desire to seek You. It is in the name of Jesus that I pray these things. Amen.

Miscellaneous Items

TUBE SOCKS

Knitting a handmade pair of socks is a labor of love. It has taken me more than 15 years of knitting to branch out and make a pair. Because this is all new to me, the best I can do so far is a pair of tube socks so I don't have to figure out how to make the heel. If you are proficient in sock knitting and want to make your sock with a heel, go for it! However, because I'm not, and this book is about patterns that are less time-consuming, I am sticking to the tube sock pattern below that my friend Patti not only made but designed as well.

Young adults love these fun and funky tube socks. The first pair I made was for my daughter. After she went off to college, I knitted for her less and less. But when she was 22, I took her to a local textile fiber festival, where she chose yarn for me to make her a pair of socks. Since she hadn't done that in years, it was a motivator for me to learn how to make these tube socks. Can you think of a young person in your life who would appreciate this colorful, encouraging gift?

SKILL LEVEL ♡ ♡ ♡ ♡

MATERIALS

Size US 3 or 4 (3.5 mm) 40- or 47-inch circular needle

100 grams of sock yarn, your color of choice, that can be machine washed and dried; divide equally into two 50-gram balls

1 skein red sock yarn to be used for the toe and the top ribbing, divided into 2 balls (you don't have to divide this equally)

Food scale (optional, but it helps to divide the yarn equally)

Stitch marker

Row counter

DIRECTIONS

This pattern is K using the magic loop method, knitting 2 socks at a time from the toe up. ▪

With red yarn, for each sock, CO 16 stitches, 8 on each needle. You will have 8 stitches on your top needle and 8 stitches on your bottom needle for both socks. This is why you need to divide your yarn into 2 different skeins. You will use one skein for each sock.

Rnd 1: K.

Rnd 2: K all stitches, except KFB on the first and last stitch of this rnd. You will now have 10 stitches on each needle.

After you knit one complete rnd for both socks (Rnd 2), PM on that first sock so you will know which sock you have knit as well as having equal rnds. When your stitch marker is on the right, you will know that you have knit a complete rnd.

Repeat Rnds 1 and 2 until you have a total of 20 stitches on each needle. I like to use a stitch marker so that I know when I am on an even rnd, which is an increase rnd.

CARE INSTRUCTIONS

Machine wash in cool water; tumble dry on low heat.

After you have your 20 stitches, K 3 more rnds in the red and then switch to MC. You will K in MC until you get toward the end of each skein or until the sock hits right below your knee or to the desired length. The ones in the photo are 15 inches in length from toe to cuff. You will switch to the red yarn for your top ribbing for 1½-2 inches. You will need a stretchy BO method. ◼◀ BO and weave in ends.

Your socks are now ready to give to someone special! Attach your gift tag.

Don't let anyone look down on you because you are young, but set an example for the believers in speech, in conduct, in love, in faith and in purity.

1 Timothy 4:12

Dear Lord, please lead me to a young adult who needs some encouragement for standing firm in her morals and values in a society that mocks and condemns her for wanting to remain pure. I ask that she not give in to the temptations that swirl around her in our unbelieving society. Give her the strength and courage to be able to live out 1 Timothy 4:12. It is in the name of Jesus that I pray these things. Amen.

Pocket Tissue Holder

*I*f you live or have lived in Texas or even visited the Lone Star State, you know how bad the ragweed pollen is. Because the Dallas/Fort Worth metroplex is a haven for seasonal allergies year-round, I like to carry these pocket tissue holders in both my purse and my car console.

Can you think of someone like me who is always blowing their nose and sniffling due to their allergies? Every time they use this nifty holder, they will be reminded of you and how you prayed for them as you made them this gift.

This is a good project for leftover yarn. One thing I like about using scrap yarn is that I am reminded of the initial gift I made with it. This particular color combination was used to make a Chemo Do-Rag.

While I had the allergy sufferer in mind when I made this pattern, I also thought about the tears that may have been shed by the person who received my Chemo Do-Rag—whether they were tears from the diagnosis or the pain from their treatments. The tissue holder could be a companion gift to go along with a Chemo Do-Rag.

SKILL LEVEL ♡

MATERIALS

Size US 8 (5 mm) straight needles

Worsted weight yarn, red*

Worsted weight yarn, your choice for the main color*

Yarn needle

*I used leftover yarn from other projects for both colors.

CARE INSTRUCTIONS

Machine wash in cool or warm water; air dry or tumble dry on low.

DIRECTIONS

Using the red yarn, CO 20 to 22 stitches. If you get your pocket tissue from a dollar store, it is smaller than the name-brand ones, so you will need to CO 20 stitches to account for the smaller size tissues.

Switch to MC yarn. Row 1 will become the RS of your piece. K until your piece measures 6 inches. Then switch to the red yarn and K 1 row.

BO and weave in the ends. (I prefer cutting a separate piece of yarn to sew the sides.)

With the RS of the piece facing up, fold in the sides of the red edging 1½ inches on each side to the middle of the piece. Sew up each short side of your project with your MC yarn. Using the red yarn, sew up 1 inch of the middle of the red to close up the opening a bit. Weave in the ends. Turn your piece right side out and stuff with your pocket tissues. Attach a gift tag.

The righteous person may have many troubles, but the LORD delivers him from them all.

Psalm 34:19

Dear Lord, I thank You that You are the ultimate Healer. From cancer to allergic rhinitis, You hear our prayers. I ask that the person who receives this gift will be reminded of Your love for them each time they pull out a tissue to blow their nose or wipe their eyes. It is in the name of Jesus that I pray these things. Amen.

FELTED MONSTER
ICE POP SLEEVE

As I am typing this, Texas is experiencing record-heat days. When it's 110 degrees outside, an ice pop can really hit the spot. These felted ice pop holders are the perfect way to get to know some of the children in your neighborhood or community. For instance, our church had a movie night for the community. Had I thought of this ahead of time, I could have knocked on the doors of my neighbors who I knew had young children and delivered these along with the card advertising our movie night.

These could also be a fun way to invite neighbor children to vacation Bible school (VBS). One of my neighbors, who has young children who love the Lord, would jump at the opportunity to be able to invite friends to their church's VBS. What a fun way for them to do that! This is an easy project that I could do with them. It uses a spool knitter and scraps of wool yarn.

SKILL LEVEL ♡

MATERIALS

12-peg round loom (flower loom)

100% wool worsted weight scrap yarn, red

Scrap yarn in your choice for the main color

Plastic googly eyes (your choice on what size)

Fabric glue

Loom hook

CARE INSTRUCTIONS

Hand-wash in cold water; air dry.

DIRECTIONS

With double strands of red yarn, CO using the e-wrap method. K 2 rnds in red. Switch to double strands of MC for Rnds 3-12. Switch back to double strands of red yarn for Rnds 13-14.

BO using the basic BO in the rnd. ■◣

My piece was approximately 4 x 2 inches before felting. If you haven't felted before, see the instructions on page 11 for felting. Glue on some googly eyes and use a bit of scrap yarn to make a mouth. Attach your gift tag with a safety pin and deliver to children in your neighborhood with some frozen ice pops!

Jesus said, "Let the little children come to me, and do not hinder them, for the kingdom of heaven belongs to such as these."

Matthew 19:14

Dear Lord, thank You for young hearts that love You and want to share the gospel with those who may not know You. Be with them as they make these fun gifts. Lead the children and their parents to knock on the right doors when inviting others to church. It is in the name of Jesus that I pray these things. Amen.

WALKER WOOLIE

*W*hen my mother-in-law was alive, she enjoyed knitting with me at the assisted living facility where she resided. Every week we would have "Knitting Club" with some of the other ladies who lived there. A majority of the residents had rolling walkers either in red or blue. I couldn't tell you how many times a resident with memory problems would wander off with someone else's walker.

I thought, *I bet I could knit something for some of these ladies.* I came up with the idea to make what I call a "Walker Woolie." The first one I made with furry yarn. It was a big hit, and I had others asking for them after that. If someone tried to go off with a walker that had a Walker Woolie, they didn't get far before the rightful owner brought it to their attention.

If you are in a knitting group, this is a great opportunity to use some of your leftover yarn stash. As a group make these "woolies" to take to one of your local senior assisted living centers. Not only do the residents enjoy receiving these handmade gifts, but they also love having new visitors.

SKILL LEVEL ♡

MATERIALS

Size US 10 (6mm) straight needles

Your choice of bulky yarn for the main color or double strands of worsted weight yarn*

Bulky red yarn or double strands of worsted weight red yarn*

Sticky Back Velcro for Fabrics, or miscellaneous buttons

I used Hobby Lobby's I Love This Chunky yarn.

CARE INSTRUCTIONS

If using the Velcro, make sure you have the Velcro closed before putting it in a zippered bag to wash. Machine wash in cool water; tumble dry on low. Or hand-wash in the sink and leave to air dry.

DIRECTIONS

Using the red yarn, CO 18 to 22 stitches (or whatever it takes to measure 6 inches wide). K for 1 row. Switch to MC.

There is no science in making this, but the average walker handle is approximately 6 inches in diameter and the black padded piece is usually around 12 inches in length.

The entire piece is K in garter stitch to make it stretchy. When your piece is approximately 11 to 12 inches in length, on the RS of your piece, switch back to the red yarn, K 2 rows, and BO.

Note: When you are finished, space out the Velcro or buttons. Velcro is easiest for an elderly person to remove the piece if it needs to be washed. However, with that being said, you have to be careful what yarn you use with it. If I am using a yarn that has more fuzz, I have to use buttons and not Velcro. Because the yarn is so stretchy, there is no need to make button holes. Attach your gift tag.

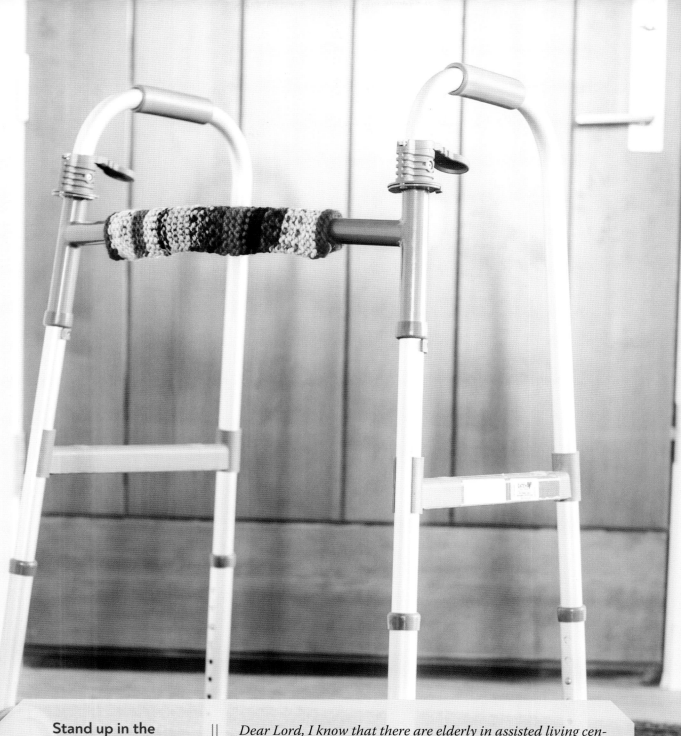

Stand up in the presence of the aged, show respect for the elderly and revere your God. I am the LORD.

Leviticus 19:32

Dear Lord, I know that there are elderly in assisted living centers who feel neglected and forgotten by their loved ones. I ask that You lead me to those who need to be reminded that even though their earthly family may have abandoned them, You never will. It is in the name of Jesus that I pray these things. Amen.

Runner's Towel

Do you know someone who is a veteran runner or perhaps someone who is new to running? I have been a runner for several years. With the Texas heat, though, I really don't want to sweat any more than I have to, so I have avoided running during the summer months.

However, at my gym, one of the trainers started a weekly running club. I started going to it because that is a way I can guarantee that I run one day a week. Being part of this group both motivates and holds me accountable for our weekly runs.

A few of the people in the club are avid runners. I noticed one of them had a microfiber towel pinned on her shirt and thrown over her shoulder. She calls it her "cape." It is a little too wide for my liking, so I decided to come up with my own version I could share with our group.

The trainer who started this group is not a runner, so this has been a challenge for him. I really appreciate that he has gone outside his comfort zone by starting this group. He will even show up at 6:30 a.m. on his day off to join us. To show my appreciation, he will be the first to receive one of these towels. I know when he uses it at his first race, he will be reminded of the prayers lifted on his behalf.

SKILL LEVEL ♡

MATERIALS

Size US 10 (6 mm) straight needles

Cotton yarn in red, and your choice for the main color*

4-inch piece of ¼-inch black braided elastic

Black thread and sewing needle (to tack elastic to towel)

I used Hobby Lobby's Crafter's Secret Cotton for both colors.

CARE INSTRUCTIONS

Machine wash in warm water; tumble dry on medium heat.

DIRECTIONS

With the red yarn, CO 28 stitches. K one row and then switch to MC.

This project is K in garter stitch, so K all rows until your piece measures approximately 12 to 13 inches. On the RS of your piece, switch to your red yarn.

After switching to the red yarn, K 2 rows.

BO. Weave in ends.

Fold the 4-inch piece of elastic in half. Sew the elastic onto one of the corners of your towel. This enables you to loop your towel through the elastic to attach to your shirt at the shoulder. ▶ Throw the towel over your shoulder for a "mini cape" that you can use to wipe your face when needed. Attach a gift tag.

I have fought the good fight, I have finished the race, I have kept the faith.

2 Timothy 4:7

Dear Lord, I ask that You bless the person who will receive this gift. I pray for safety and endurance as they run. No matter what is going on in their life, I pray that they have the faith to know that You are faithful. When the runner finishes the race that they have been training for, may the athlete remember the best prize of all is Your grace and mercy given to them through the blood of Christ. May Your child be reminded of this as he/she uses this towel. It is in the name of Jesus that I pray these things. Amen.

CAMERA STRAP COVER

o you frequently notice a relative at family functions or a friend at sporting events or activities who always carries a nice camera? Is there someone you know who takes pictures professionally or is an avid photographer? This strap cover is a nice accessory and reminder that you notice and appreciate their photo-taking skills.

What amazes me about the art of photography is how a person can be so gifted to capture something that the average eye doesn't see. A while ago, I had a photographer take some pictures of me for my blog. Before she even met with me, she talked with me on the phone for over an hour. She said it helps her to get to know the person before she meets for a photo shoot. She wanted to know my heart.

Whether it is someone who has professionally taken photos for you or a parent you see on the sidelines at sporting events, this gift will encourage your photographer friend to keep pursuing their passion and sharing it with others. When you give this camera strap cover, it lets this person know how much you appreciate their gift of photography.

SKILL LEVEL ♡ ♡

MATERIALS

4 size US 3 (3.25 mm) 5-inch double-pointed needles

1 skein 4-ply superfine wool blend yarn, red*

1 skein superfine wool blend yarn, your choice for main color*

*I used a self-striping sock yarn that had red in it, so I only needed one skein of yarn for this project. I used Patons Kroy Socks yarn.

CARE INSTRUCTIONS

Machine wash in cold water, delicate cycle; air dry or tumble dry on low heat.

DIRECTIONS

My strap was made to fit my daughter's Nikon. Its wider center portion (the part with the words "Nikon" on it) length was 22 inches, so I made mine 23 inches, adding 1½ inches of ribbing at both ends to help the strap cover stay in place. I have no idea if all camera straps are the same length, so you might have to measure the strap you plan to cover to confirm it. (You don't have to tell them you are making something for them.)

If you are using a self-striping sock yarn that has red in it as I did, you will need to find the start of a red stripe to CO using the red portion of the yarn. With the red yarn, CO 28 stitches. Divide evenly between 3 needles. (I divided the stitches 9, 10, 9.)

K2P2 for ribbing for the first 1½ inches. (For the yarn I was using, that ended up being two color changes. My red portion was not 1½ inches; it was whatever my stripe length was for the yarn.) If you are using a separate skein of red yarn, K the 1½ inches of ribbing all in red and then switch to the MC. For me this was 13 rnds of the ribbing. The ribbing portion will make it fit snug around that smaller leather portion of the strap.

You will continue to K in the rnd until your piece measures approximately 21½ inches.

Luckily for me, my self-striping yarn was exactly where I needed it for that last 1½ inches of ribbing to end with the red portion. If you can see that your self-striping yarn is not going to end with a red portion, then you will need to cut your yarn and find the red to add for the end. If you are using a different skein for the red color, then you will need to switch to that yarn once your piece measures the 21½ inches.

K2P2 for the last 1½ inches. For me, it ended up being 12 rnds, and I did my BO on rnd 13.

BO and weave in your ends.

The total length of the strap cover I made, with the ribbing on both ends, was 23 inches. When I was finished, I sprayed it with water and pressed with a warm iron to smooth it out. Make sure you put a thin towel between your yarn and iron before you do this. If you have the camera, slip it on. If not, include an explanatory note and attach your gift tag to the strap.

The LORD said to Samuel, "Do not consider his appearance or his height, for I have rejected him. The LORD does not look at the things people look at. People look at the outward appearance, but the LORD looks at the heart."

1 Samuel 16:7

Dear Lord, I pray that the person I give this strap to sees the value of their profession or hobby. In this world of Snapchat, Facebook, Instagram, and Twitter, taking photos with an actual camera is becoming a lost art. Help them to showcase Your majesty and glory in the photos they take. As they take their pictures, help them to see through Your lens and capture the beauty You see in every person. It is in the name of Jesus that I pray these things. Amen.

CABLED
BOOT TOPPERS

*B*eing a young girl in this fast-paced world can be a real struggle. She is bombarded with worldly views that tell her what is not acceptable in God's eyes is okay. It is easy for the lines to become blurred between what is right and what is wrong.

Do you know a tween or teen who is being tempted to run with the wrong crowd? Are you praying for the prodigal child of yourself, a friend, or family member?

Consider making these boot toppers to share with a young lady who needs to be reminded to make good friendship choices. If you are involved with youth in some capacity, I am sure someone has already come to your mind as you read this.

SKILL LEVEL ♡♡♡

MATERIALS

Size US 10 (6 mm) straight needles

1 skein worsted weight acrylic or acrylic blend yarn in red*

1 skein worsted weight acrylic or acrylic blend yarn, your choice for the main color*

Cable needle

Yarn needle

Row counter

I used Lion Brand Heartland for both colors of yarn.

CARE INSTRUCTIONS

Machine wash in cold water, delicate cycle; air dry or tumble dry on low heat.

DIRECTIONS

(worked in multiples of 11)

Sizes: small, medium, and large. Directions are for the small size. Directions for the medium and large sizes are in parentheses.

With red yarn, CO 44 stitches for the small size (medium: 55, large: 66).

Row 1: *P1K1*; repeat to end of row.

Row 2: *K1P1*; repeat to end of row.

Row 3: *P1, K1*; repeat to end of row.

Row 4: *K1, P1*; repeat to end of row.

Change to MC yarn for Rows 5-19.

Row 5: *P3, K8* 4 times, ending with a P3.

Row 6: *K3, P8* 4 times, ending with a K3.

Row 7: *P3, cable 4 forward (slip 4 stitches onto your cable needle, hold in front of your work, K4 from your working needle, and then K the 4 stitches from your cable needle)*, repeat 3 more times, ending with P3.

Row 8: *K3, P8*; repeat to end of row.

Row 9: *P3, K8*; repeat to end of row.

Row 10: *K3, P8*; repeat to end of row.

Row 11: *P3, K8*; repeat to end of row.

Row 12: *K3, P8*; repeat to end of row.

Row 13: *P3, K8*; repeat to end of row.

Row 14: *K3, P8*; repeat to end of row.

Row 15: P3, *cable 4 forward (slip 4 stitches onto your cable needle, hold in front of your work, K4 from your working needle, and then K the 4 stitches from your cable needle)*, repeat 3 more times, ending with P3.

Row 16: *K3, P8*; repeat to end of row.

Row 17: *P3, K8*; repeat to end of row.

Row 18: *K3, P8*; repeat to end of row.

Row 19: *P3, K8*; repeat to end of row.

Rows 20-24: Switch to the red yarn. Work in K1P1 ribbing for remaining rows.

BO in pattern; sew up seam. Weave in ends. Attach your gift tag.

Whether you turn to the right or to the left, your ears will hear a voice behind you, saying, "This is the way; walk in it."

Isaiah 30:21

Dear Lord, I pray for this young lady to be influenced by positive peer pressure and to have godly friends who make wise choices. I ask that You protect her against negative peer pressure and poor judgment that will result in harmful consequences. Help her to be grounded in her faith so that she will be able to resist temptations and the pressure to sin. Open her eyes to be able to recognize, detest, and run from sinful behaviors. It is in the name of Jesus that I pray these things. Amen.

YOGA MAT STRAP

*Y*oga has been part of my workout routine for more than 15 years. At first, I had a hard time with it because of the whole "Namaste" and bowing your head thing. Rather than do that at the end, I bow my head and say a silent "Amen." It is a way for me to both honor God and my body as well.

Not only is yoga a form of exercise, but the classes also form a sense of community between the students and teacher. I once tore a shoulder muscle and was unable to go to my regular yoga class for nearly a year. It was hard to believe how much I missed seeing the teacher and classmates.

Because the people in the class are more acquaintances than friends, you may not know their religious beliefs. You will definitely be stepping outside of your comfort zone when you give away your gift, but that's what faith is all about. Is there a class regular who always uses a mat provided by the classroom? You can purchase an inexpensive yoga mat at a discount store and place one of these handmade straps around it to give as a gift. You can also make a DIY small spray bottle of yoga mat cleaner to go with your strap.

SKILL LEVEL ♡

MATERIALS

Size US 7 (4 mm) straight needles

50/50 cotton/acrylic blend yarn in red and your choice for the main color*

Yarn needle

Stitch marker

Cascade Avalon is a good yarn to use for this project.

CARE INSTRUCTIONS

Machine wash in warm water, delicate cycle; tumble dry on low.

DIRECTIONS

Using the red yarn, CO 10 stitches.

P1, K8, P1 for 4 inches.

Switch to MC (this will be the RS). I like to place a stitch marker on the RS of the piece so I know when to switch back to my red yarn at the end.

Continue in P1, K8, P1 for 42 inches. When the MC portion is 42 inches (46 inches including the red part), on the RS of your piece, switch back to the red yarn and continue in P1, K8, P1 for the last 4 inches.

BO. From CO to BO edge will be 50 inches in length and 2 inches wide.

With the RS facing up, fold in the red portion of your piece 2 inches and sew down to form a small loop. Repeat on the other side. This will

form the 2 loops needed on each end. Weave in ends.

To form the loops to go around your yoga mat, take one of the red loops and pull it through the other red loop. Pull that down to one end. Take that loop you just made and pull it through the other end loop and slip it down to the other end. It is now ready to secure your rolled yoga mat. ◼◁ Attach your gift tag.

Note: A nice touch is to include a small spray bottle of yoga mat cleaner along with the strap. You can make it yourself by filling a small spray bottle with distilled water and put a few drops of lemongrass essential oil in it.

Don't you realize that your body is the temple of the Holy Spirit, who lives in you and was given to you by God? You do not belong to yourself, for God bought you with a high price. So you must honor God with your body.

1 Corinthians 6:19-20 NLT

Dear Lord, I don't know whether or not this person in my exercise class knows You. If she is an unbeliever, I ask for a mustard seed of faith to be planted in her soul. If she already knows You, then I ask that You draw her closer to You. Every time she goes to class, remind her of Your unending love. It is in the name of Jesus that I pray these things. Amen.

119 HAPPY ARE ALL ... low the laws of God.

who search for God, and alwa...
rejecting compromise with evi...
ing only in his paths. You have ...
your laws to obey—, oh, how I wa...
follow them consistently. Then I will...
be disgraced, for I will have a clean ...
After you have corrected ...
thank you by living as I ...
Oh, don't forsake ...
into sin ag...

to the Lord and
me. He is for
hat can mere
on my side,
o hate me
an to put
ake ref-
g!
world
ban-
and

Seed Stitch Bookmark

Several years ago, I was invited to join a book club. Because my main pursuit is knitting, I really don't do a whole lot of reading on the side unless I am sitting by a pool. This means I usually read only one or two books a year. Nonetheless, the mother of one of my son's friends asked me to join her annual book club Christmas party.

They seemed like a fun group of ladies, so I decided to step out of my comfort zone and try reading one book a month with them. This was a totally new experience for me, and I read books I never would have read with women I might not have met otherwise.

I created this bookmark pattern to honor these special women. I plan to give each one a bookmark at our next Christmas gift exchange. While I initially thought that being a member of a book club would last only a year, my membership has surpassed my expectations.

Regrettably, I had to withdraw from the club for a year. However, when I ran into one of these ladies at the gym, she encouraged me to come to their next get-together. I did not realize how much I had missed this group until I was with them again.

Do you belong to a book club or know a book lover you could bless with the gift of a bookmark? This is a quick and easy project to make, and you can use scrap yarn, if you choose. You can even tuck the bookmark in a favorite book of yours and give it as an especially personal and meaningful gift.

SKILL LEVEL ♡♡

MATERIALS

Size US 3 (3.25 mm) straight needles

Light worsted weight (DK) yarn, red

Light worsted weight (DK) yarn, your choice for main color

Row counter

Crochet hook

CARE INSTRUCTIONS

Hand-wash in cold water; lay flat to dry.

DIRECTIONS

Using the red yarn, CO 9 stitches.

Rows 1-2: K.

Row 3: Switch to MC yarn; K.

Row 4: K1P1 to end of row. (This begins the seed stitch pattern where you K on the P stitches and P on the K stitches.)

Continue in the seed stitch pattern until your piece measures 5 to 6 inches (if you would like this to accompany a smaller book, start the decrease at 5 inches).

You will start your decrease as follows:

Row 1: K2tog, K1, P1, K1, P1, K1, P2tog. (7 stitches)

Row 2: P1, K1, P1, K1, P1, K1, K1

Row 3: K2tog, P1, K1, P1, K2tog. (5 stitches)

Row 4: K1, P1, K1, P1, K1

Row 5: K2tog, K1, K2tog. (3 stitches)

BO these 3 stitches. Weave in ends.

With red yarn, cut four 10-inch pieces of yarn to serve as fringe on the tip of your bookmark. Fold the 4 pieces in half and use your crochet hook to hook them through the end of the bookmark for fringe. ◼️ Attach your gift tag.

Your word is a lamp to guide my feet and a light for my path.

Psalm 119:105 NLT

Dear Lord, I pray for these women to not only read books for pleasure but to also study Your Word and hear the Good News about Jesus Christ. Let Your Word be a lamp to guide their feet and a light to direct their paths. I thank You for placing women in my pathway so that I can experience and share life with them routinely. For those who may not have personally felt Your peace and joy, I ask that You open their hearts to seek what only You can give. It is in the name of Jesus that I pray these things. Amen.

About the Author

Lisa Hennessy is the author of the blog *Knit Pray Share*, where she combines her love for knitting and her strong faith in God to inspire others to do the same. Because of her inability to sit still, knitting is a form of therapy to help her relax and calm her anxiety. As she knits, she's able to pray and take her focus off any problems before her and fix her eyes on Jesus.

She has both her BA and MS in speech communications. She lives in the Dallas/Fort Worth area with her husband and is mother to two adult children. In her spare time, when she doesn't have a pair of needles or a pen in her hand, you can find her at the gym or running a 5k.

You can connect with Lisa at

www.KnitPrayShare.com

Knit, Pray, Share

@knitprayshare

@knitprayshare